THE ANTIETAM JOURNAL

Vol. VI
March 2024

Kevin R. Pawlak
Editor

A Publication of the Antietam Institute

ISBN-13: 979-8-218-38273-5

Editorial Advisory Board

The Antietam Journal is a biannual publication of the latest research, interpretation, and stories of the Maryland Campaign of September 1862 that highlights the participants involved—soldier and civilian—and the lasting impact of the campaign on American history.

The Antietam Institute was established in 2021 as a member-based, educational, and philanthropic 501(c)(3) non-profit organization. The Institute educates the public on the central role of the Maryland Campaign of 1862 and Battle of Antietam as a major turning point of the Civil War that directly resulted in the issuance of the preliminary Emancipation Proclamation. Antietam Institute-sponsored conferences, symposiums, publications, and leadership forums facilitate collaborative learning and knowledge exchange, create unique opportunities for discovery and inspire further historical research.

Manuscript Submissions

Send manuscript submissions to the editor at editor2@antietaminstitute.org. Feature articles should be approximately 10,000 words in length (including footnotes).

Cover image: Courtesy of Kevin R. Pawlak.

Table of Contents

The Editor's Column
by Kevin R. Pawlak

For a campaign that to this day carries so much importance in American history, one might be tricked into thinking there is nothing new to learn or see related to the Maryland Campaign and the Battle of Antietam. I was reminded of this a couple of weeks ago when I received the opportunity to walk Federal artillery positions on the south end of the battlefield. This land is still privately owned, but it easily offers the best view of the Antietam battlefield I have ever seen. The entire field and all its prominent landmarks were there before me in one glance. It was a stark reminder of the vastness of Antietam's story, and that there is always more to learn.

This latest edition of *The Antietam Journal* is filled with more stories and information about the campaign. Our feature articles show the breadth of Antietam's history. Steven R. Stotelmyer, recent author of the Antietam Institute's latest book-length publication, takes a deep look at Robert E. Lee's health during the campaign and how it may or may not have affected his generalship. Wilson Beebe's next article carries us to the postwar period and provides a perspective on the scope of work undertaken by the Antietam Battlefield Board and its historian, Ezra Carman, to interpret and preserve the Antietam battlefield.

Author James A. Rosebrock is back with an excerpt from the Maryland Campaign diary of a Confederate artillerist. Jim is *the* artillery historian of the Battle of Antietam. Be sure to read this article and get a copy of his *Artillery of Antietam* if you do not already have one.

Brian Wyland shares the personal story and effects of Wilson Colwell, an officer in the 2nd Wisconsin Infantry. Colwell, like countless other common soldiers, deserves to have his story told, and Wyland has done that nicely.

Once you are done reading this edition of the journal, take it with you out into the field. J. O. Smith provides a useful guide to sites to see related to the September 12-15, 1862, Battle of Harpers Ferry.

The leading authority on that battle and the campaign and a leading preservationist of the western Maryland landscape, Dennis Frye, is the subject of our Institute Interview.

Make your voice heard in the growing conversation of the Maryland Campaign. Do you have an article you would like to write for a future issue of *The Antietam Journal?* Or, let us know what you think of this publication that is now in its sixth volume. Just send an email to editor2@antietaminstitute.org. I look forward to hearing from you!

Kevin R. Pawlak

Antietam Institute Announcements

From Frederick to Sharpsburg: People, Places, and Events of the Maryland Campaign Before Antietam

We are pleased to announce that the Institute's latest publication, *From Frederick to Sharpsburg: People, Places, and Events of the Maryland Campaign Before Antietam*, by Steven R. Stotelmyer, has been released. Steve is a distinguished author of the Maryland Campaign. He is a native of Hagerstown, Maryland, served in the U.S. Navy and holds a master's degree from Hood College. Steve helped form the Central Maryland Heritage League in 1989 which was successful in preserving part of the South Mountain Battlefield. He is the author of *The Bivouacs of the Dead: The Story of Those Who Died at Antietam and South Mountain*, and most recently *Too Useful To Sacrifice: Reconsidering George B. McClellan's Generalship in the Maryland Campaign from South Mountain to Antietam*.

Antietam Institute Historical Research Center

We live in a digital age with thousands of sources at our fingertips. Unfortunately, there is rarely one place to go to find everything we are looking for. The Antietam Institute's website is now home to the Historic Research Center, a repository to collect and share digital copies of historical and contemporary material about the Battle of Antietam and the related Maryland Campaign.

The Historical Research Center has sources grouped into three categories: unit histories, images, and documents. This is a living resource that will continue to have sources added to it, so continue to visit the page to find more resources. Visit the Historical Research Center at https://antietaminstitute.org/hrc/s/HRC/page/welcome to find these valuable resources or to submit some of your own items for inclusion in this exciting digital resource.

"The Commanders of Antietam" Speaker Series in the Pry Barn

Institute historians are back at the Pry House this summer for our "Commanders of Antietam" speaker series. Come to the Pry House to hear the contributors of the *Commanders of Antietam* discuss in detail some of the commanders that fought in the 1862 Maryland Campaign. The series is sponsored by the Antietam Institute and hosted by the National Museum of Civil War Medicine. The presentations begin in the Pry Barn at 2:00 p.m. and is a pay-what-you-please event. There is a $3.00 suggested donation to tour the Pry House Field Hospital Museum. Visit our website for a complete schedule.

The Pry House is open from 11 a.m. to 5 p.m. on Saturdays, from June 1 through October 26. The Pry House Field Hospital Museum is located at 18906 Shepherdstown Pike, Keedysville, MD 21756.

Commanders of Antietam

We are pleased to announce that our Membership incentive book for 2024 will be *Commanders of Antietam*.

Commanders of Antietam, the Union and Confederate Commanders at the Battle of Antietam is a comprehensive look at the biographies of both armies' high command during the Maryland Campaign of September 1862. This treatment focuses on the lives of Union and Confederate commanders from the brigade level up to the army commanders, Robert E. Lee and George B. McClellan.

Each commander's biography is broken into three sections: Before the Maryland Campaign; During the Maryland Campaign; and After the Maryland Campaign. This is the most complete volume of commanders' biographies in the Maryland Campaign.

This book has been written by a collaboration of Antietam Battlefield Guides, National Park Service Rangers and volunteers, and Civil War historians. Kevin Pawlak and Brad Gottfried are the editors of this volume. It is the third in a series of books focused on different aspects of the campaign, including *Brigades of Antietam* (edited by Bradley Gottfried) and *Artillery of Antietam* (by James A. Rosebrock), both published by the Antietam Institute.

Experience Antietam

Join us this summer for a series of weekly members-only battlefield excursions called "Experience Antietam." These two-hour programs on Wednesday evenings will be led by Antietam Institute historians and will cover seminal parts of the battlefield over the course of nine weeks. In addition to the Cornfield, the Sunken Road, and the Burnside Bridge, excursions will focus on the fighting in the East Woods, the West Woods, actions at the Middle Bridge and the Final Attack. Find out more at: antietaminstitute.org/experience-antietam-hikes/.

Lee's Delicate Condition
by Steven R. Stotelmyer

"The three weeks covered by the Maryland expedition have been the most criticized of Lee's entire military career...his decision to accept battle on the 17th, and, still more, his determination not to leave Maryland the night after the battle have been said to exhibit an infirmity of judgment he disclosed at no other time." –Douglass Southall Freeman[1]

There is an overlooked aspect of Confederate operations in Maryland during September of 1862 that often remains unmentioned in popular history. General Robert E. Lee, one of the most iconic figures of the Civil War, suffered a debilitating physical injury just prior to his entry into Maryland. If Lee's injuries are mentioned at all in the popular histories of the campaign, they are usually given short shrift. One of the results of this perfunctory treatment is that the popular image of the bold, audacious Confederate general remains largely intact, while the actual picture of an aging invalid unable to take care of himself, mostly remains overlooked. Furthermore, how Lee's injuries may have affected his

U.S.A. Ambulance typical of those captured and used by C.S.A. Due to the primitive suspension, travel in an ambulance for Lee aggravated his pain because of the constant bumping and jolting. (Library of Congress)

---

1 Freeman, *R. E. Lee, A Biography*, 2:409-10.

decisions and controversial actions during the campaign have generally been ignored.

After the Battle of Second Manassas, during the early hours of August 31, 1862, in the vicinity of the Stone Bridge over Bull Run on the Warrenton Turnpike, General Lee participated in a meeting with his two chief lieutenants, generals James Longstreet and Thomas "Stonewall" Jackson. As best can be determined from the many and varied accounts, Lee had dismounted from his horse to confer with his subordinates when suddenly an alarm was sounded that Yankee cavalry was at hand. The resultant noise and confusion caused his horse to shy, and as Lee moved to grab the reins, he tripped and landed heavily on both outstretched hands. As a result of the fall, he severely sprained both wrists and broke at least one bone in his right hand. According to Henry W. Thomas, with the 12th Georgia Infantry, "Lee had his hand hurt *very painfully* by his horse, and Dr. N. S. Walker, surgeon of the Forty-fourth Georgia, dressed his wound and gave him a bottle of liniment, which greatly relieved him." It is uncertain if Dr. Walker placed splints on Lee's hands at this time. However, within a few days, both hands were splinted, bandaged to the fingertips, and the right arm supported in a sling. If the veracity of Maj. Walter H. Taylor, Lee's adjutant general, can be trusted, "He had no use of either hand, and for some days each arm had to be carried in a sling."[2]

Major Gilbert Moxley Sorrel, Longstreet's chief of staff, provided one of the most candid descriptions of Lee's condition at the beginning of the campaign:

> General Lee suffered a painful accident...his hands were badly damaged; one had a small bone broken and the other was nearly as bad with the twist and strain. Both were put into splints, but were painful and most uncomfortable. For some time the saddle had to be given up and the ambulance called into use.[3]

---

2 Harsh, *Confederate Tide Rising*, 205-07; Henry W. Thomas, *History of the Doles-Cook Brigade* (Atlanta, GA: Franklin Printing and Publishing Company, 1903), 469 (italics by Stotelmyer); Walter H. Taylor, *General Lee, His Campaigns in Virginia; 1861-1865 With Personal Reminiscences* (Norfolk, VA: Nusbaum Book and News Company, 1906), 115.
3 Gilbert Moxley Sorrel, *Recollections of a Confederate Staff Officer* (New York, NY: The Neale Publishing Company, 1905), 102-03.

On September 2, as the Army of Northern Virginia marched to Leesburg, Virginia, Sgt. Maj. Richard T. Dodson, with the Stuart Horse Artillery, noticed a group of dismounted officers standing on a knoll by the roadside. As Dodson recalled:

> Among them was General Lee, whom I now saw for the first time since in Richmond, a year before...Now I beheld him so greatly changed...He had recently had a fall from his horse, caused by the stumbling of the animal, and had badly sprained both wrists. They were now done up in splints, which, covering the hands, were bound around with white clothes. He stood with arms crossed upon his person, watching the troops as they passed...He presented to them, who loved him, so pathetic a figure, a victorious chieftain, yet a defenseless man.[4]

If a joint or tendon is wrenched or stretched beyond its normal range of movement the resultant injury is often diagnosed as a sprain. Naturally, the injury's severity depends on how badly the ligaments are torn. In Lee's case, it appears that when his outstretched hands hit the ground, the force of the impact bent them back towards his forearms much too far. Lee's accident apparently resulted in acute pain, swelling, and some loss of function, making it more severe than average. These injuries, though not life threatening, placed noticeable limitations upon the Confederate commander. He was forced to travel in an ambulance instead of horseback because he could no longer hold the reins of his mount. This restricted his movements to locations only accessible on four wheels, not horseback. For the next several weeks Lee would require constant assistance with even the most mundane tasks, such as eating meals, dressing himself, and attending to his personal toilet.

For the most part during the Maryland Campaign, unless surrounded by familiar places and acquaintances, General Lee attempted to remain aloof and out of the public eye. It certainly is plausible that because of his injuries, he wanted to avoid embarrassment and public humiliation. One has only to imagine the spectacle of Lee, the conqueror of McClellan on the Peninsula and Pope at Second Manassas, being spoon-fed like some helpless infant to understand why the Southern commander elected to keep to himself.

---

4 Richard Townshend Dodson, "With Stuart in Maryland," undated newspaper article, NYPL, Carman Papers Correspondence Files, Box 2, Folder 5.

Apparently, one of the familiar places where Lee felt comfortable was Harrison Hall in Leesburg, Virginia. Before his entry into Maryland, he spent the night of September 4, 1862, at the home of a distant relative, Henry Tazewell Harrison. In his injured condition and with much work to do, Lee abandoned the rigors of his customary tent and accepted the desired comfort and hospitality of the Harrison household. A guard was posted, and his headquarters flag was placed at the gate. There were several children in the household, and years later one of them, Mary Jones Harrison, related incidents of Lee's visit. "An ambulance stopped by a granite stepping stone," remembered Mary, "and a soldierly figure with both wrist in splints, walked up the long Box bordered brick path, and was welcomed." Before Lee could do anything else, and at the suggestion of his host, he submitted to an examination by Dr. Samuel K. Jackson. According to Mary, "Dr. Jackson, Mrs. Harrison's Physician was called from next door to see that the wrists were dressed again."[5]

As Dr. Jackson recalled his house call:

> General Lee was quartered at my next door neighbor, Mr. Henry Harrison. On the evening of his arrival I was summoned to see him professionally. I found that he had hurt both hands by a fall...the Genl came down hard on both hands. There appeared to be a serious ligamentous strain in both & I thought a fracture in one. I made him as comfortable as possible for the night.[6]

In the days prior to modern methods of examination to determine internal damage from an injury, physicians, such as Dr, Jackson, relied upon "wrist stability" for diagnosis and treatment. Without an x-ray, Jackson depended upon Lee's ability to move his damaged limbs and bear weight without pain. No doubt, Dr. Jackson also depended heavily on the outward visible symptoms, such as swelling and discoloration. There is no way of knowing with complete certainty, but it is likely that more than a single bone in the right hand was fractured, and Lee's forearms may have suffered small hairline breaks in the radius or ulna. These types of physical trauma are commonly associated today with

---

5 Mary Jones Harrison, "General Lee's Visit to Leesburg and Harrison Hall," (SC 0048), Thomas Balch Library, Leesburg, VA.
6 Samuel K. Jackson, "Reminiscences of Genl Lee," Essays circa 1885, Manuscript Collection Mss7:1 L515:6, Virginia Museum of History and Culture, Richmond, VA.

severe wrist injury. Dr. Jackson's examination most likely was further handicapped by Lee's well-known stoicism and his ability to endure pain and privation.[7]

Lastly, there is the possibility of another side effect, beyond Lee's physical limitations, that is related to Dr. Jackson's examination and treatment: did the measures taken to make Lee as comfortable as possible include medication? And if so, what kind of medication was prescribed, and how might it have affected his acumen on the battlefield? Beyond the brief reference by the surgeon of the 44th Georgia to the bottle of liniment, the historical record is strangely silent regarding this aspect. There is no evidence to indicate that Lee was given any other medication for his pain. This does not mean that he wasn't, it just means there is nothing in the historical record to prove that he was. However, acute physical pain was a constant companion to Lee in the Maryland Campaign and there is no reason to believe that Dr. Jackson did not provide relief and comfort with medications readily available in the mid-nineteenth century. Morphine certainly was high on the list of Victorian era pain relievers. However, one cannot but think that if Lee were taking morphine, someone would have observed it and commented (or perhaps not, given the lack of any first-hand observations of him being dressed and spoon-fed by others). There was an alternate pain-relief medication in common use at the time, available at any local apothecary shop. It was a mixture of alcohol and opium called Laudanum. It also had a dilute second cousin known as Paregoric that was more accessible to the public, but it still contained opium. Both medications were common in the Victorian age and used for everything from the common headache to tuberculosis. Victorian nursemaids even spoon-fed the drug to cranky infants. Their uses were no more extraordinary or noteworthy in the mid-nineteenth century than the use of over-the-counter medications, such as aspirin and acetaminophen is today. If one looks beyond Lee the stoic icon and considers Lee the injured patient, there exists the likelihood he was treated by Dr. Jackson with some kind of common pain reliever in addition to liniment.[8]

During his stay at Harrison Hall, General Lee received a special visitor, his son Robert E. Lee, Jr., or "Bob," as Lee called him. "Lee's son Bob came to see his father," remembered Mary Harrison, "Father and son

---

7 Bradley Graham, *The Antietam Effect, The Backstory of the Antietam Campaign of 1862* (Gettysburg, PA: Media Magic of Gettysburg, 2012), 186, 200n61.

8 https://en.wikipedia.org/wiki/Laudanum, accessed April 26, 2022.

talked together in the northeast corner of the library." The two men did not see each other again until the Battle of Antietam.

Mr. Harrison's hospitality was far famed, and the breakfast table next morning "groaned" with good things. According to Mary, "Mrs. Mathew Harrison, a cousin of the house sat on Gen. Lee's right and cut his food for him and fed him."[9]

Before Lee's departure, Dr. Jackson returned to attend to the splints and later commented he thought they "were unseemly equipment for an approaching battle." There is no doubt that when Lee entered Maryland, he did so in an ambulance with both hands immobilized in splints and his right arm supported in a sling. As Dr. Jackson noted, "He [Lee] had gone off in an ambulance, for he was unable to ride on horseback."[10]

By September 9, Lee was camped with his army south of Frederick, Maryland. Among the many civilian visitors was Mrs. Catherine Markell. Her husband, Mr. Frederick "Fred" Markell, was a prosperous local merchant who ran a dry goods store on Patrick Steet. The Markells were fervently committed to the Southern cause, and Catherine, and several others, insisted on visiting Lee. For the most part he attempted to remain aloof and out of the public eye; however, it appears Mrs. Markell was relentless in her attempt to see the general. "Gen. Lee...breaking one wrist and injuring the other," wrote Catherine. "Both [hands] were bandaged almost to the fingertips, so that we could but just touch them in shaking the noble old soldier's hand. 'Touch them gently, ladies,' he said, when we insisted on a hand shake."[11]

When the Confederate army marched out of Frederick on September 10, several eyewitnesses observed Lee riding in an ambulance. An unnamed army surgeon serving at the U.S. hospital on South Market Street observed, "During their passage I saw Lee riding in an ambulance, he having been recently injured." Civilian observers described Lee's vehicle in more common terms. Mrs. Virgie Brown often told stories from the family history handed down to her from her mother, Mary

---

9 Harrison, "General Lee's Visit to Leesburg and Harrison Hall," Thomas Balch Library, Leesburg, VA.

10 Jackson, "Reminiscences of Lee," Virginia Museum of History and Culture, Richmond, VA.

11 Catherine Markell, Manuscript Diary entry, September 9, 1862, Maryland Room, C. Burr Artz Public Library, Frederick, MD; Gordon, "A Textbook History of Frederick County," Manuscript, Maryland Room, C. Burr Artz Public Library, Frederick, MD, 95; Kathleen A. Ernst, *Too Afraid to Cry: Maryland Civilians in the Antietam Campaign* (Mechanicsburg, PA: Stackpole Books, 1999), 33-34, 45.

Quantrell. As Virgie related, "My mother was standing on the front porch when the Confederate troops came marching out west Patrick Street leaving Frederick...Gen. Lee came by in his carriage."[12]

Perhaps the most amusing anecdote regarding Lee's mode of travel on September 10 came from Mr. Ezra Burkhart of Fairview, a small village west of Frederick near the passage of the National Road over the Catoctin Mountains. In 1884, Mr. Burkhart was known by local citizens for a story he told about Lee:

> I was down in Mexico during the Mexican War and saw General Lee down there...I did not see him again until just before the battle of South Mountain. Lee was lying in an ambulance, with his head sticking out of the rear end. The ambulance stopped in front of my house, under a big shade tree. Lee saw me and recognized me immediately...We talked awhile and then the ambulance drove on.[13]

On September 12, Lee and part of his army moved to Hagerstown, Maryland. Their march took them through the village of Funkstown. Angela K. Davis, a local resident, observed, "General Lee, who was an elegant looking gentleman, passed through town in a very common ambulance." Davis further noted the Palmetto flag of the state of South Carolina floating over the ambulance. In addition, the ambulance was accompanied by a guard of six soldiers "armed to the teeth." Angela also observed Lee with his arm in a sling and somehow attributed it to his "having been wounded by a stray shot from one of his own soldiers." One noteworthy detail may be deduced from Mrs. Davis' observations: due to his riding in an ambulance with bandaged hands and an arm in a sling, rumors of Lee being somehow wounded were not uncommon.[14]

---

12 Unknown, "Doc. 202, The Rebel Army in Frederick, Accounts by an Army Surgeon," *The Rebellion Record, A Diary of American Events* (New York, NY: G.P. Putnam,1864), 11 vols., Frank Moore, ed., 5:607; Virgie Quantrell Brown, "Heroine of Whittier, Real Barbara Fritchie and Her Mythical Deed," *The Washington Post*, March 27, 1900.

13 Charles C. Kaufman, "Tells of Experiences During the Civil War," *Middletown Valley Register*, February 8, 1929.

14 Angela Kirkham Davis, "War Reminiscences: A Letter to My Nieces Emma K. Devlin, Belle K. Page, and Leigh K. Williams," Typescript, 30. Special Collections Research Center, Syracuse University Libraries, Syracuse, NY.

On the morning of September 14, Gen. Lee was unexpectedly forced to return to Boonsboro, Maryland, and his footsore soldiers were forced into battle at South Mountain. Throughout much of the day, Maj. Gen. D.H. Hill's lone division defended the two northern gaps against two Union army corps. As if it were some period melodrama, Maj. Gen. James Longstreet arrived with his command just in time and proceeded to send them immediately to Hill's relief. As Longstreet's chief of staff remembered, "We happily got to Hill just as he was being driven from the crest of the mountain, and in time to save him." Due to his injuries Robert E. Lee was not on the battlefield of South Mountain. It was one of the few times in the war the Army of Northern Virginia was without the presence of Lee on a battlefield. "Lee sent his staff officers to ascertain the situation," wrote Lee's biographer Douglas Southall Freeman, "in his crippled condition he did not attempt to direct the battle."[15]

General Lee's absence on the battlefield did not mean he chose to remain out of sight. Lee took a prominent position dismounted and standing along the roadside at the western foot of the mountain where he was visible to the troops as they passed. "I arrived with the rear of the column at the base of the ridge, where I found General Lee standing by the fence, very near the pike," wrote Brig. Gen. John B. Hood. "I dismounted, and soon stood in his presence." This is borne out by Chaplain George G. Smith of the Phillips' Georgia Legion. Smith had stopped off in Funkstown for breakfast and was attempting to find his regiment. "I found Generals Lee, Longstreet, and Jones, standing at the base of the pass."[16]

After the battle, at a meeting with his subordinates in a private home at the foot of the mountain in the eastern outskirts of Boonsboro, General Lee inquired about the prospects for continuing the fight. General Longstreet deferred to Gen. D.H. Hill, who was more familiar with the situation. Hill flat out stated that the toehold the Confederates retained at Turner's Gap was untenable, as the enemy had turned the position and held the high ground. Longstreet was in favor of a withdrawal, and Hill saw no alternative to an immediate retreat. Apparently, because he had not been on the field, Lee could not bring himself to believe this was the

---

15 Sorrel, *Recollections of a Confederate Staff Officer*, 105; Freeman, *R. E. Lee, A Biography*, 2:372.

16 Hood, *Advance and Retreat*, 39; George G. Smith, "A Fighting Chaplain," *Camp-Fire Sketches and Battlefield Echoes 61-65*, W. C. King, W. P. Derby, eds. (Springfield, MA: King, Richardson & Co., 1888), 148.

case without further proof. Before he would order a retreat, Lee insisted that a small detachment go back to ascertain if the Federals still held the high ground. A picket officer, Lt. W.P. Dubose, of the Holcombe Legion, was charged with the duty, went back to the position, and was immediately captured. Furthermore, a Union prisoner provided information that two more Federal army corps were on the march for Turner's Gap. Consequently, Lee acquiesced to his subordinates' suggestions and ordered the retreat. How much time was lost due to Lee's evident doubting of Longstreet and Hill is unknown; however, as Col. P.F. Stevens, commanding the Holcombe Legion, did not receive Lee's order for the reconnaissance back to the gap until "11 or 12 o'clock," some time was obviously lost.[17]

As early as 10:00 a.m. the following morning, September 15, Maj. Gen. George B. McClellan reported to General-in-Chief Henry Halleck, "Information this moment received completely confirms the rout and demoralization of the rebel army. General Lee is reported wounded." By 8:00 a.m. that morning several of McClellan's subordinates and scouts had debriefed civilians in Boonsboro. No doubt, even though the retreat was conducted in darkness, due to Lee's appearance and his mode of travel, it was rumored after the Battle of South Mountain by civilian observers (just like Mrs. Davis in Funkstown a few days earlier) that Lee was wounded. Furthermore, Col. Charles Marshall, Lee's aide-de-camp, clearly remembered when Lee left Boonsboro, "he was riding in his ambulance, and I rode in front guiding him through the troops, artillery, and trains." Therefore, it is absolutely certain General Lee was still using the ambulance on September 15 when he entered Sharpsburg.[18]

The next day, September 16, Lee abandoned the ambulance and returned to horseback. Apparently, if there was going to be battle at Sharpsburg, he did not want a repeat of his experience at South Mountain. However, both hands were still bandaged (and possibly still in splints) and the right arm still in a sling. Consequently, Lee was forced to spend his time either walking or riding for brief periods with an aide leading his mount by the reins.

---

17 Carman, *The Maryland Campaign*, 1:368; William P. Dubose, "William Porcher Dubose Reminiscences," 93-96, Southern Historical Collection, University of North Carolina, Chapel Hill NC. See also Col. P. F. Stevens' report, OR 19/1:942, for the disappearance of his adjutant, Lt. Dubose.

18 OR 19/2:294-95; Charles Marshall to Ezra A. Carman, November 22, 1900, Carman Papers Correspondence Files, Box 3, Folder 1, New York Public Library, New York.

Although no contemporary source provides a precise date for Lee's return to horseback, there is a postwar regimental history of the New Orleans Washington Artillery that places him out of the ambulance and walking in the streets of Sharpsburg on September 16. Lieutenant William M. Owen wrote in 1885, "Riding through the town [Sharpsburg], to find Gen. Longstreet, I met Gen. Lee on foot." Owen's postwar observation definitely shows Lee had left the ambulance for travel on foot; however, his next phrase opens up another controversy. According to Owen, while Lee was walking, he was "leading his horse by the bridle." Because General Lee's right arm was in a sling, Owen's observation must be interpreted to mean Lee was using his left hand to hold the reins as he walked.[19]

Some authors claim that the issue of what Lee could grasp with his left hand during the Battle of Antietam has caused unnecessary debate.[20] However, it is only through a thorough examination of the issue that an accurate representation of Lee the human being, not Lee the mythical icon, emerges in the history of the battle. The dispute surrounding General Lee's ability to use his left hand on September 17 is at the heart of the controversial hallowed image of the audacious Confederate chieftain taking the bridle and fighting through the pain versus the truthful picture of the aging invalid being led by someone else holding the reins.

Two other postwar accounts have been offered as proof supporting the claim that Lee personally took direct control of his mount by holding the reins. One comes to us from James Dinkins with the 18th Mississippi Infantry. In 1897, in a book of personal "Recollections," Dinkins noted that while his regiment was going into battle in the West Woods, "we passed General Robert E. Lee. He sat on his horse near a battery of the Richmond Howitzers, which was actively engaged. We cheered him as we passed." Seven years later, in the pages of the *Southern Historical Society Papers*, Dinkins related the same story with a slightly different twist: As the regiment passed Gen. Lee, Dinkins noted, "General Lee...was riding a little black horse, and halted near a battery which was

---

19 William Miller Owen, *In Camp and Battle with the Washington Artillery of New Orleans* (Boston, MA: Ticknor, 1885), 141.
20 Alexander B. Rossino, *Their Maryland: The Army of Northern Virginia from the Potomac Crossing to Sharpsburg in September 1862* (El Dorado Hills, CA: Savas Beatie, 2021), 215n7.

actively engaged. The Mississippians yelled, and General Lee, reining his horse about, watched us go by."[21]

The other postwar account comes from Col. John B. Gordon, the commander of the 6th Alabama Infantry at Antietam's infamous Bloody Lane. In his 1904 *Reminiscences of the Civil War*, Gordon wrote that during a short lull before the combat in the lane, "General Lee took advantage of the respite and rode along his lines on the right and centre." The same account (more or less) appeared ten years earlier in the pages of a Confederate veteran's publication. The article dealt with a previous address made by Gordon to the group. Gordon is reported to have told those in attendance of his experiences at Sharpsburg where, "Gen. Lee rode up to my command."[22]

Regarding Dinkins' postwar claim about Lee "reining" his mount, if we were to doubt his veracity, we would not be the first. In preparation for his comprehensive postwar manuscript on the Maryland Campaign, Antietam historian Ezra A. Carman corresponded with James Dinkins regarding the movements of his regiment and brigade. According to Thomas G. Clemens, editor of the three-volume study of Carman's manuscript, "Dinkins may not be a reliable source, and Carman seemed to ignore his more outlandish claims." If Dinkins ever mentioned a mounted Lee holding the reins to Carman, Carman chose not to use it.[23]

The two passages from Gordon used in support of Lee taking direct control of his mount make no mention one way or the other about Lee actually holding the reins. Both accounts, one by Gordon and the other attributed to him, only relate that Lee "rode" the horse. One can just as easily ride a horse with somebody else leading it by the reins (especially if one still has a painfully injured wrist). Gordon, in an article in the same publication nine months earlier, is alleged to have stated he held the reins. In a review of another lecture by Gordon there appeared this noteworthy sentence: "He [Gordon] mentioned the loyal devotion of the speaker to his chief, and recited the incident of his taking Lee's bridle reins in the battle of Sharpsburg." In all three accounts by Gordon of Lee on horseback, the only direct reference of anyone holding the reins of Lee's

---

21 James Dinkins, *1861 To 1865. Personal Recollections and Experiences in the Confederate Army by an Old Johnny* (Cincinnati OH: The Robert Clarke Company,1897), 59, "The Griffith-Barksdale-Humphrey Brigade, and Its Campaigns," *SHSP*, (1904), 32:262.

22 John B. Gordon, *Reminiscences of the Civil War* (New York, NY: Scribner and Sons, 1904), 84; *Confederate Veteran*, vol. 2, no. 9 (September 1894), 2:272.

23 Carman, *The Maryland Campaign*, 2:200n46.

mount is to Gordon himself. It would seem that Gordon actually refuted the claim of Lee taking direct control.[24]

All three of the preceding writers, Owen, Dinkins, and Gordon penned their anecdotes after Lee's death in 1870. Therefore, Lee was not around to either affirm or deny the veracity of those statements regarding his holding the reins. However, two of Lee's relatives, his nephew and his son, were very much alive at this time and able to refute the veracity of these claims. Brigadier General Fitzhugh Lee commanded a brigade of Confederate cavalry in his uncle's army during the Maryland Campaign. In 1894, he wrote about his relative's mode of travel at Antietam: "Most of the time he was on foot...He was obliged to ride in an ambulance or let a courier lead his horse. In the tumult of battle he could ride but little along his lines."[25]

Robert E. Lee, Jr., may be the most reliable source regarding his father's injuries. Before the Battle of Antietam "Bob," as Lee senior called him, last saw his father at Harrison Hall in Leesburg shortly before the start of the campaign. He was quite familiar with General Lee's injuries, as father and son were briefly reunited during the battle on September 17:

> General Lee was dismounted with some of his staff around him, a courier holding his horse...I went up to speak to my father. When he found out who I was, he congratulated me on being well and unhurt...He was much on foot during this part of the campaign, and moved about either in an ambulance or on horseback, with a courier leading his horse.[26]

While it is also true that both Bob, and his cousin Fitzhugh, wrote after Lee's death, it cannot be denied they were intimately aware of his mode of travel throughout the campaign. It is difficult to doubt their veracity, especially the genuineness of a son's memories of his father on a battlefield.

If the controversy over Lee's use of his left hand was just a matter of whether or not he was able to hold the reins of his horse, we could end

---

24 Gordon, *Confederate Veteran*, vol. 2, no. 1 (January 1894), 2:2.
25 Fitzhugh Lee, *Great Commanders: General Lee* (New York, NY: D Appleton and Company, 1894), 210.
26 Robert E. Lee, Jr., *Recollections and Letters of General Robert E. Lee* (New York, NY: Doubleday, Page and Company, 1904), 78.

here; however, there is more. In his regimental history, Lieutenant Owen made another controversial claim regarding Lee's use of his left hand at Antietam:

> While standing with Col. Walton in Squire's battery, about noon, Gen. Lee walked over to us. One hand was in a sling, it not having recovered from the accident at second Manassas; the other held his field-glass.[27]

Lieutenant Owen does not represent a singular source, there are several. After the war, Maj. Gen, James Longstreet stated that during the battle, "General Lee and I stood on the top of the crest with our glasses, looking at the movements of the Federals." Brigadier General John G. Walker also commented, "As I passed what is now known as Cemetery Hill, I saw general Lee standing erect and calm, with a field-glass to his eye." Maryland Campaign chronicler Ezra A. Carman wrote, "he [Lee] saw, by aid of his glass." Taken as a whole, these statements would seem to prove the claim that Lee was able to hold either binoculars or a telescope, or both.[28]

Some have offered the explanation that if Lee was using a "glass," an aid was holding the instrument for him. This explanation gains strong support in light of another postwar anecdote by John A. Ramsay. During the battle, Lt. Ramsay served with Manly's (North Carolina) Battery. Around mid-afternoon, near the southern outskirts of Sharpsburg, while observing "a large number of straggling soldiers" they met General Lee:

> General Lee seeing Lieutenant Ramsay's telescope, said to him: 'What troops are those?' pointing to the position occupied by Captain Reilly's battery on the day before. Lieutenant Ramsay drew his telescope from the case and handed it to General Lee. He held up his wounded hand (fingers in bandages) and said: '*Can't use it.* What troops are those?'[29]

---

27 Owen, *In Camp and Battle*, 150.

28 James Longstreet, "The Invasion of Maryland," *B&L*, 2:671; John G. Walker, "Sharpsburg," *B&L*, 2:676; Carman, *The Maryland Campaign of September 1862*, 1:392.

29 John A. Ramsay, "Additional Sketch Tenth Regiment," *Histories of the Several Regiments from North Carolina*, 5 vols., Walter Clark, ed. (Raleigh, NC: R.M. Uzzel, Priner and Binder/Nash Brothers, 1901), 1: 553, 575 (italics by Stotelmyer).

Lieutenant Ramsey's language regarding Lee's bandaged fingers is almost an exact match of Mrs. Markell's observation of bandages to the fingertips eight days earlier in Frederick. If Ramsay's account has any veracity, it certainly seems doubtful Lee was holding any type of "glass" at Antietam. However, we do not have to rely on the observations of others regarding the use of Lee's left hand. We may arrive at a final judgment based upon the words of Lee himself in a letter to his wife in mid-October 1862:

> My hands are improving slowly, and with my left hand, I am able to dress and undress myself, which is a great comfort. My right is becoming of some assistance, too, though it is still swollen and sometimes painful. The bandages have been removed. I am now able to sign my name. It has been six weeks today since I was injured, and I have at last discarded the sling.[30]

If Lee's statement regarding the six weeks is accurate, it places the date of his letter on October 12, about three and one-half weeks after Antietam on September 17. Also noteworthy, beyond Lee's admission that the bandages had finally come off, is his statement that his right hand was becoming useful again. That Lee was not yet fully recovered six weeks after his accident is borne out by his wartime aide, Charles Marshall. In postwar correspondence with Antietam historian Ezra A. Carman, Marshall wrote that Lee, in consequence of his injuries, "was unable to use his bridle arm for more than two months."[31]

Wrist and hand injuries are among the most painful, distracting, and slowest to heal. Average wrist sprains may take two to ten weeks to heal, with more severe cases taking longer. That splints were initially prescribed for Lee meant the injury was not average, and the recovery period may have been somewhere between six to twelve weeks. For argument's sake we will set aside Dr. Jackson's observation that the injury was severe, since we have the patient's own observation. Lee and Marshall's statements are consistent with the recovery time for a severe injury. So is Lee's language about the healing being slow, considering his age. Lee was fifty-five years old in 1862. This is important because the human body's capacity to heal itself diminishes with age. Indeed, in older

---

30 Lee, as cited in Lee, Jr., *Recollections and Letters of General Robert E. Lee*, 79.
31 Marshall to Carmen, November 22, 1900, Carman Papers Correspondence Files, Box 3, Folder 1, New York Public Library, NY.

people, wrist and hand injuries, like those of Lee, may never heal completely. Furthermore, if a person uses a severely sprained wrist in some type of strenuous activity (such as reining a horse) before it is properly healed, they prolong the healing process and risk further or permanent damage. Had Lee done so and further aggravated the injury, it is improbable he would have been able to use the hand to dress himself by October 12. His mention that the right hand was still swollen and painful is also consistent with a severe injury. Finally, the fact that according to Lee, the bandages and sling were finally removed on October 12, certainly implies they were still in place on September 17.[32]

This prompts the heretofore unmentionable question regarding the influence of Lee's injuries on his ability to process information and formulate coherent decisions. Pain, sleep deprivation, exhaustion, and embarrassment were constant companions of Robert E. Lee during the Maryland Campaign.

Diagnoses of diminished mental capacity without clinical examination is a slippery slope, but a few generalizations may be drawn from Lee's experience after his accident. Any attempted use or movement of his arms, wrists, and hands involved pain. For most of the campaign, Lee was bouncing around in a Confederate ambulance over the roads of Maryland, and this would only acerbate the constant pain associated with his injuries. Even if we set aside the controversial side-effects of Victorian pain relievers upon cognition, there is a direct relationship between persistent pain, fatigue, and rational thinking. Despite the incessant pain, the responsibilities of leadership resulted in long days and sleepless nights. Injury and duty resulted in fitful sleep and exhaustion. As Lee's campaign began to unravel at South Mountain, his personal experience was one of further exertion, worry, stress, disappointment, and depression. Add into the mix the particular indignity and embarrassment of not being able to attend personally the simplest of human activities, such as dressing oneself, feeding oneself, attending to bodily functions oneself, and you have a recipe for impaired decision making. The psychological toll of such a debilitating physical impairment on the inner

---

32 Graham, *The Antietam Effect,* 186; Jeffrey R. M. Kunz and Asher J. Finkel, *The American Medical Association Family Medical Guide* (New York, NY: Random House, 1987), 543-44, 815; https://www.webmd.com/fitness-exercise/wrist-sprain, accessed April 15, 2022; https://myhealth.alberta.ca/Health/aftercareinformation/pages/conditions.aspx?hwid=u f7611, accessed April 15, 2022.

workings and decision-making process of a military leader such as Robert E. Lee remains one of the most profound mysteries of the campaign.

The point to be made is that it was absolutely impossible that Lee could avoid the effect of his injuries on his frame of mind in early September 1862. This is not to say that his physical impairments and their associated psychological side-effects were the sole reason for his controversial decisions, there certainly were other factors at work as well. However, as noted by author Bradley Graham, "After mentioning this incident [Lee's August 31 accident] early in their campaign narratives, authors tend to ignore the injury, the throbbing wrist seeming to disappear as a factor worth considering while the campaign unfolds."[33]

One of those in high command around Lee recognized the effects of his injuries upon his temperament. Walter H. Taylor, Lee's adjutant general, stated:

> This [Lee's August 31 accident] was a sore trial to the general's patience. The ambulance could not go into many places where a horse would have carried him, and so his movements were greatly hindered: all this in addition to the physical suffering he was experiencing.[34]

We have previously noted the impact of Lee's condition regarding the close of day at the Battle of South Mountain: His absence from the battlefield and the resultant delay related in the decision to retreat towards Sharpsburg.

It has long been noted by those who tend to venerate Lee that the Maryland Campaign of 1862 seems to be the exception to the rule. Douglas Southall Freeman, Lee's premier biographer, made special note of this conundrum:

> The three weeks covered by the Maryland expedition have been the most criticized of Lee's entire military career. His strategy in invading Maryland has been assailed; his division of the army for the capture of Harpers Ferry has been condemned as rash and unsoldierly; his dispatch of Longstreet to Hagerstown instead of keeping him with D.H. Hill on the march westward from Frederick has been held responsible for

---

33 Graham, *The Antietam Effect*, 186.
34 Taylor, *General Lee*, 115-16.

failure at Boonsboro; his decision to accept battle on the 17th, and, still more, his determination not to leave Maryland the night after the battle have been said to exhibit an infirmity of judgment he disclosed at no other time.

It certainly must be recognized that an element of this "infirmity of judgment," or diminished mental capacity, on Lee's part, coincided with his physical infirmities that resulted from the accident just prior to his entry into Maryland.[35]

Perhaps no other aspect of the Maryland Campaign than the movement back into Virginia and the resultant Battle of Shepherdstown better illustrates Lee's infirmity. As Lee communicated to his president on September 25, "When I withdrew from Sharpsburg into Virginia, it was my intention to recross the Potomac at Williamsport, and move upon Hagerstown." No other decision made by Lee during the campaign best demonstrates how out of touch Lee was regarding the condition of his army and its capabilities at the time. The Army of Northern Virginia suffered its greatest casualty rate for a single day at Antietam. In addition to the casualties, there were large numbers of stragglers. Indeed, the total number of stragglers exceeded more than fifty percent of the casualties. The army was in no condition for further operations. Regardless, it is fruitless to speculate how many men Lee could have carried with him back across the Potomac at Williamsport, since the question is moot because the Battle of Shepherdstown brought an end to any hopes of continuing his campaign.[36]

It is at Shepherdstown on September 20 that we find some of the most damning statements regarding Lee's diminished mental capacity by participants and historians. About daybreak, Lee arrived at the headquarters tent of Gen. D.H. Hill and his aide, Maj. James W. Ratchford, inquired about the location of General Jackson. "Lee seemed unable to summon his usual powers of decision," wrote Hill's biographer Hal Bridges, "he was suffering from exhaustion brought on by inadequate rest and nervous tension." Hill asked Lee repeatedly what he should do; finally, Lee replied. "I do not know what to tell you, but follow Jackson." All well and good, but Hill did not know Jackson's location. After the war, Ratchford recalled the conversation and said of Lee, "I never saw a man more confused." Hill, in a letter to Jackson's biographer, Rev. R.L.

---

35 Freeman, *R. E. Lee, A Biography,* 2:409-410.
36 OR 19/2:626; Harsh, *Sounding the Shadows,* 213-14.

Dabney, stated, "I have never seen him [Lee] exhibit such indecision and embarrassment." It is hard to imagine that the return to Virginia did not also entail a return to the ambulance with all its associated restrictions upon Lee's movements. Regarding Lee's confusion on September 20, historian Joseph L. Harsh, speculated, "One last time during the campaign, Lee's lack of personal mobility frustrated his ability to make personal observations and to exert direct control."[37]

There are postwar anecdotes that place Lee on the battlefield of South Mountain. We know conclusively he was not. There are postwar anecdotes that have General Lee holding a "glass" at Antietam. We have his own purported admission that he could not. There are postwar anecdotes that have Lee in the saddle holding the reins of his horse on September 17. We have statements from his nephew and son that he did not. Nonetheless, the popular image of Robert E. Lee in Civil War history has been carefully cultivated over the years.[38] In the history of the Maryland Campaign there are two opposing images to choose: The cultivated, iconic portrayal of the bold and audacious Confederate general fighting through the pain of his injuries and personally taking direct control versus the iconoclastic picture of an aging invalid, unable to take care of himself and limited by the physical restrictions imposed upon him. In the final analysis, it may have been the latter, and not the former, that had a more crucial influence on Lee's failed campaign.

---

37 Hill and Ratchford as cited in Hal Bridges, *Lee's Maverick General: Daniel Harvey Hill* (New York, NY: McGraw-Hill Book Co., 1961), 128; Harsh, *Taken at the Flood*, 463-64.

38 Thomas L. Connelly, *The Marble Man, Robert E. Lee and his Image in American Society* (Baton Rouge, LA: Random House, Inc. 1977), 3-4. The postwar anecdotes of James Longstreet and John G. Walker that have Lee holding a "glass" may represent deliberate, or accidental, participation in the iconic cultivation of Lee's postwar image. Walker's *Battle & Leaders* writings of Lee have been thoroughly examined and discredited by Joseph L. Harsh. See *Taken at the Flood*, 134-45, and *Sounding the Shallows*, 217-18.

"He was much on foot during this part of the campaign, and moved about either in an ambulance or on horseback, with a courier leading his horse." Robert E. Lee, Jr. (Author)

"Without Praise and Without Censure": Ezra Carman and the Antietam Battlefield Board, An Appreciation by Wilson Beebe

When at last it was over, when the immensity of the quietude spilled into a second day, when the Confederate Army had left its lines and retreated south across the Potomac, the remaining soldiers, citizens, teamsters, reporters, nurses, and camp followers paused in the course of their duties and preoccupations to look upon the landscape of history—the carcasses of horses and the corpses of men; spent shells and discarded rifles; the litter of forage caps, clothing, cartridge boxes, canteens, haversacks, blankets, bayonets, shoes, boots, spurs, and harnesses; smashed artillery pieces, splintered caissons, and broken wagons.

While blind to the violence yet to be endured, they understood that the war had indeed been engaged, and that whatever else one made of it, the forces of the rebellion had been repulsed from their invasion of the North. If more significance was wanted, Abraham Lincoln's issuance of the Emancipation Proclamation in just a few more days would give the outcome further claims on the attention of posterity.[1]

Thus began the memory of Antietam.

In possession of the field, federal engineers and surveyors fanned out across the countryside, mapping the landscape and sketching the battle lines as they understood them. Reporters elaborated on their first sketchy dispatches. The literate volunteers of 1861 and 1862 wrote home. Those at home read the letters and the newspapers.

Corps, division, brigade, and regimental commanders prepared their official reports, sending them up the chain of command by the hundreds. In all, the documentation of the Battle of Antietam (and the actions at South Mountain and Harpers Ferry) contained in the *Official Records of the War of the Rebellion* would eventually compose some 2,000 pages, beginning a dialogue that would continue for another 50 years and be supplemented by thousands of pages more.

---

1 Allen C. Guelzo, *Lincoln's Emancipation Proclamation* (New York: Simon & Schuster, 2004),153-157. The battle was on Wednesday, September 17; the Confederates were gone from their lines on the morning of Friday, September 19; Lincoln released the Preliminary Emancipation Proclamation on Monday the 22nd; it was in the newspapers starting the following morning.

Among those engaged in the memorialization of Antietam was Ezra Ayers Carman, a colonel of the Thirteenth New Jersey Volunteer Infantry, who had led his men through the East Woods and into the firefight in the Miller cornfield. Three months later, having secured comfortable quarters in the vicinity of Sharpsburg, he commenced what was to become a lifetime's endeavor: "completing a good map of the Antietam battle and a full account of the action."[2] Soon after the battle, this business manager from Newark, New Jersey, and one of the founders of the New Jersey Historical Society, began his work by "touring" the field and collecting information from residents, Confederate prisoners, and soldiers still camping in the vicinity.[3]

Starting in 1866, Carman served as New Jersey's appointee to the board of trustees of Antietam Cemetery. Twenty-eight years later, his early initiative and avocation would bear fruit in an appointment to the Antietam Board itself, the official government custodian of the battlefield story.[4] Carman would be instrumental in the creation of the official tactical history as manifest in the iron War Department tablets that continue to mark the field to this day and in the *Atlas of the Battlefield of Antietam.*

The Antietam Board was charged in 1891 with the responsibility for "surveying, locating and preserving the lines of battle of the Army of the Potomac and of the Army of Northern Virginia at Antietam,"[5] and consisted at first of two persons appointed by the Secretary of War: Col. John C. Stearns of Vermont, who had seen Union service, and Henry Heth of Virginia, a former Confederate major general.

The Board's efforts began with the obvious: the *Official Records*, the material relevant to Antietam having been published in 1887 by the Government Printing Office. The Board soon found, however, that many of the reports contained in Volume 19 contributed little to the Board's charge of marking the lines of battle with a fair degree of precision and

---

2 Ezra Ayers Carman, Ezra Carman Diary, Ezra Carman Papers (Manuscript Group Series No. MG-1761) New Jersey Historical Society, Newark, NJ, quoted in John Connor Scully, "Ezra Carman, Soldier and Historian," thesis, George Mason University, 1997, 1.
3 Scully, "Ezra Carman," 32-37.
4 Scully, "Ezra Carman," 92.
5 H.R. 10830, 51st Cong., 1st session, June 7, 1890, quoted in Charles W. Snell and Sharon A. Brown, *Antietam National Battlefield and National Cemetery, Sharpsburg, Maryland: An Administrative History*, ts., U.S. Dept. of the Interior, NPS, Washington, D.C., 1986, 69.

specificity. It is one thing to read Brig. Gen. John Gibbon's account of the Fourth brigade's advance down the Hagerstown Pike, which is really quite full of referent detail. It is another to go to the pike and ask, exactly, "where?" It is then that the abundance of referent detail becomes curiously more relational and difficult.

Of such reports, one of the early students of Antietam, Francis Winthrop Palfrey wrote:

> They are very numerous, and many of them are not short, but they hardly ever tell to what point of the compass the faces of the troops were turned, and the indefinite article is constantly used. A lane, a road, a fence, a wall, a house, a corn-field, a piece of woods, such are the constantly recurring phrases which constantly baffle and disappoint the curious student.[6]

Invariably, the formal documentation of a battlefield invites these questions of exactness, both because the context of the land demands it, and because, for those for whom the battle was a defining moment in their lives, the essential narrative cannot be communicated without reference to the ground on which it occurred. An approximate verisimilitude will not do.

* * *

Nowhere was that drive for specificity more pronounced than in the question of the location of the mortal wounding of Twelfth Corps commander Gen. Joseph K.F. Mansfield. The story of Mansfield's death, one of six general officers killed that day, became the particular provenance of Maj. John M. Gould of the 10th Maine, which was brigaded under Mansfield's Twelfth Corps. Gould, author of the *History of the First-Tenth-Twenty-Ninth Maine Regiment*, and of an 1877 book on recreational camping and walking, corresponded regularly with veterans, the Antietam Board, and Carman.

By the time Carman joined the Antietam Board in 1894, the fray concerning the location of Mansfield's death had been engaged in earnest at least since 1891, with the principal antagonist to Gould's position being

---

6 Francis Winthrop Palfrey, *The Antietam and Fredericksburg, Campaigns of the Civil War* (New York: Scribner, 1882), 74-75.

the 125th Pennsylvania Volunteers, as articulated by Thomas McCamant, formerly a lieutenant in Company G of that regiment. The 125th believed that General Mansfield was wounded in front of their lines and assisted to the rear by their men. Major Gould's position was that the General's wounding was in front of the 10th Maine, which "Gen. Mansfield in person piloted … into the East Woods" before taking the bullet that killed him, and that it was men of the 10th Maine that came to his assistance.[7]

Both accounts are filled with expressions of certainty, calls to witnesses, and the offering up of corroborating testimony. The 125th Pennsylvania's case depended on locating the 10th Maine on its immediate left at the moment of Mansfield's wounding rather than where Gould placed the 10th Maine, which was forward of the 125th and on the northern perimeter of the East Woods, and at a not inconsiderable distance of some three or four hundred yards.

The "10th Maine was at our left when General Mansfield rode forward to reconnoiter, for I recollect (in company with Lieutenant Shallenberger of Company I.) of conversing for a few moments with a member of your regiment as to the probabilities of a severe engagement, after our skirmishers were recalled."[8] Gould's response: "I have never been able to find a man of the 10th Maine who saw the 125th Pennsylvania that day to recognize them."[9]

The protestations of the 125th continued. In 1895, upon reading Gould's "pamphlet, styled 'General Mansfield at Antietam,'" McCamant wrote to him: "I have read it with interest, but must still say you are wrong in locating the spot where Mansfield was wounded, east of the Smoketown Road and at the point where your marker was placed in 1891."[10]

Antietam Board iron explanatory Tablet No. 27, when cast, had only a locationally anodyne reference to Maj. Gen. Mansfield's mortal wounding:

----

7 John M. Gould, statement, Nov. 3, 1892, ts., Ezra A. Carman Papers, Box 3, New York Public Library (NYPL), New York.

8 Thomas McCamant, letter to John M. Gould, March 20, 1891, ts., Carman Papers, Box 3, NYPL.

9 Gould, statement, Carman Papers, NYPL.

10 Thomas McCamant, letter to John M. Gould, June 27, 1895, ts., Carman Papers, Box 3, NYPL.

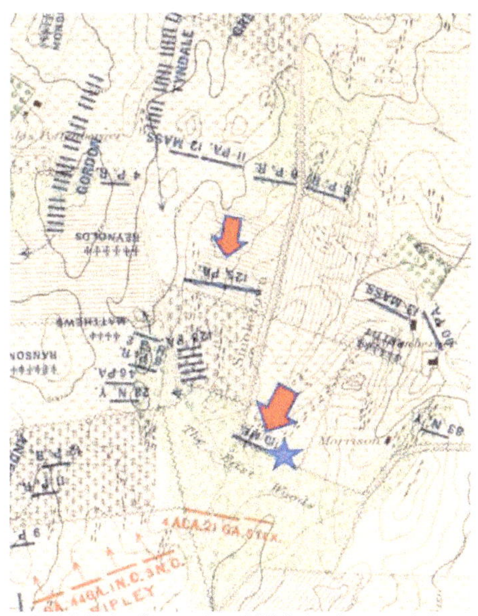

Highlight from the 1904 Antietam Atlas showing the positions of the 125th Pennsylvania and the 10th Maine on Sept. 17 at 7:30 a.m., with the Mansfield Mortuary Monument indicated as a blue star. (Author)

The Twelfth Corps left its bivouac on the Line and Hoffman farms at daylight, moved forward, in column of Battalions in mass and deployed in support of the First Corps, Williams' Division on the right and Greene's Division on the left. Its line extended from D.R. Miller's house, on the Hagerstown Pike, in a southeasterly direction to and across to Smoketown Road. While the deployment was in progress, Maj. Gen. Mansfield was mortally wounded and carried from the field.[11]

Nor did the tablet's placement, where the Smoketown Road bisects the Cornfield and the East Woods, suggest any resolution to the controversy, having been logically located with two other tablets (Nos. 28 and 29) concerning the movement of Williams' division in that general vicinity on that day.

---

11 George R. Large and Joe A Swisher, *Battle of Antietam: The Official History by the Antietam Battlefield Board* (Shippensburg, PA: Burd Street Press-White Mane Publishing Company, 1998), 72.

It wasn't until 1896, when marking the locations where general officers had fallen, that Carman resolved the question.[12] He placed the Mansfield mortuary monument where Gould's research said it should be and is where the State of Connecticut also erected its own monument to Mansfield in 1900. This determination, dependent as it was on validating the locations of the 125th Pennsylvania and the 10th Maine, was further borne out in the *Atlas* when published in 1904, showing the 10th Maine to be on the northern perimeter of the East Woods when Mansfield was shot, with the 125th Pennsylvania to its right and significantly to its rear.

Alas, for the 125th—while there were "yet surviving members ... who witnessed the wounding of General Mansfield ... that can and will, if necessary, make affidavit that General Mansfield was mortally wounded at least one hundred and forty yards to the right front of the monument recently erected to his memory by the State of Connecticut"[13]—time ran out, and the research and advocacy of John Gould won Carman's concurrence.[14]

* * *

Considering the magnitude of the forces engaged and the vagaries of recollection, it is not difficult to see the obstacles precision documentation of the battle was likely to encounter. Even with the action broken down into the obvious—the formal organizational components of each army—the information management demands of the project were immense, confronting eight corps or commands, divided into 30 divisions, further subdivided into over 100 brigades and battalions, and atomized into more than 500 regiments and batteries.

Where were they, what did they do, and when did they do it?

Compounding the problems of information complexity and volume was the passage of time. The documentary process of the Antietam Board did not even begin until 30 years after the battle, contemporaneous with the emergence of the cultural trend in the remembrance, documentation, celebration, and commemoration of the war. It was then that

---

12 Susan Trail, "Remembering Antietam: Commemoration and Preservation of a Civil War Battlefield," diss., U. of Maryland, 2005, 225.

13 125th Pennsylvania, unidentified author, ts., Carman Papers, Box 3, NYPL.

14 Carman believed that at least part of the Mansfield controversy was the result of the course of the Smoketown Road having changed after the war. Scully, "Ezra Carman," 144-145.

reminiscences and accounts flooded the journals of veterans' groups and filled the pages of newspapers and magazines, among them the very popular Century Magazine and its series *Battles and Leaders of the Civil War*. It is this same period that corresponds with the rise, decline, and eventual resurrection of the Grand Army of the Republic (GAR), the great fraternity of Union veterans and, in its latter days, the principal lobby for veteran's pensions.[15]

The Antietam Board had access to all this material, and if some of it was a poor source of exactitude, or altogether dubious, it was a rich source of potential correspondents. The antidote to ambiguity was the painstaking assessment of unit locations, movements, and actions based on the recollections of company, regimental, brigade, and division commanders, or any of the other 90,000 combatants. The Board began by circulating a form letter to elicit such input, chiefly by asking each respondent to give their unit locations in relationship to other units, a method which provided at least some relational verification.[16]

Other informants were solicited through notices placed in newspapers in both the North and South, listing units of interest to the Board, and asking former members to contact it to provide information necessary to complete its understanding. The assistance the Board received was of varying quality. In corresponding with Major Gould in 1898, Carman observed that:

> ... out of 100 letters written I get replies to about 50 and
> of the 50 not more than 4 or 5 are of any value. It takes

---

15 Stuart McConnell, *Glorious Contentment: The Grand Army of the Republic 1865-1900* (Chapel Hill: UNC Press, 1992).
16 Antietam Board, Carman Papers, Box 3, NYPL.

"Dear Sir: Acting under Act of Congress, to mark the lines of the Battle of Antietam, and having ascertained that you were engaged in that battle, we will thank you if you will kindly furnish us the following:--

What regiments were on your right, left, front, and rear during the night of September 16, 1862?
Where was your command on the morning of September 17, 1862, when the battle was begun?
How far did you advance in direction of the enemy during the battle?
It is our duty to try to secure all the evidence we can from every intelligent officer or enlisted man who was at Antietam, hence this letter."

more trouble to eliminate myths than to get solid fact. I have had much experience at collecting battlefield reports, but Antietam goes ahead of all.[17]

Battlefield visits were also a part of the process, conducted as unit reunions, by specific invitation of the Board, as part of state delegation visits, and sometimes as personal pilgrimages. These too were oftentimes of doubtful value as Carman related in this instance of the Ohio Commission.

> The rain fell in torrents every hour of their stay and I am squarely soaked through. I don't know anymore now than I did before they came, but they did know more than the Pennsylvanians and confirmed my ideas.[18]

What is more, the propensity of memory to reinforce mistaken impressions was reinforced by a landscape that, with time and the seasons, changed in subtle ways, and which had wanted for natural geographic landmarks to start with.

> The woods, cleared land, fences, wheat and corn fields, which constituted points of reference, at the time of the battle, have been modified and changed in the intervening years so as to make it a matter of extreme difficulty to identify them in any case; while in some, if not many cases, such identification is impossible.[19]

Some of the correspondents were diffident at best about entering into the discussion of what had happened so many years ago, were skeptical of what they themselves could contribute, and of the accuracy of the contributions of others. Francis Barlow wrote: "For more than thirty years, I have been occupied as a lawyer, and have paid no attention

---

17 Ezra Carman, letter to John Gould, May 28, 1898, Antietam Collection, Dartmouth College Library, quoted in Scully, "Ezra Carman," 102.

18 Ezra Carman, letter to Maj. George B. Davis, Dec. 13, 1894, Antietam Battlefield Board Papers, Series 706, Record Group 92, National Archives, quoted in Scully, "Ezra Carman," 105.

19 Maj. George B. Davis, letter to Secretary of War Daniel S. Lamont, Oct. 4, 1894, Series 706, Records Group 92, National Archives, quoted in Snell and Brown, "Administrative History," 87.

whatever to these historical matters, and, indeed, have read very little that has been written upon the subject." In encouraging the Board to compare the accounts of generals Miles and Longstreet, he expressed the opinion that:

> ... some light may be obtained as to the position of the troops and the condition of things in that part of the field. It is in this accidental and incidental way that the truth of battles and campaigns can be most accurately determined, for I have little confidence in official reports.[20]

By contrast, in debunking the claim that General Lee had considered retreating during an alleged Council of War on the night of September 17, General Longstreet wrote Carman:

> I beg leave to add that the official accounts are the only reliable source of information of the war and its battles. All accounts post bellum make should be taken with a grain of salt, and unless supported by other and reliable persons or by circumstances that justify faith, should be salted away.[21]

Palfrey, on the other hand, expresses a substantial amount of skepticism concerning official reports, especially Southern ones, having found "the doubt growing upon him whether they were made primarily for the information of the superior officers who were entitled to receive them, or for publication in local newspapers and the glorification of the writers."[22]

*　*　*

---

20 Francis Barlow, letter to the Antietam Board, May 20, 1893, Carman Papers, Box 3, NYPL.

21 James Longstreet, letter to Ezra Carman, Feb. 11, 1897, ts., Carman Papers, Box 3, NYPL.

22 Palfrey, "Antietam and Fredericksburg," 115.

On the stationary of Smith & Connors, Plumbers and Gas Fitters, James Smith wrote from Cleveland, Ohio.[23]

Jacob N. Cox, as Dean of the Faculty, responded on the letterhead of the Law School of the Cincinnati College.[24]

W.H. Taylor, corresponding in February of 1892, wrote as the President of the Marine Bank of Norfolk, Virginia.[25]

They wrote the Antietam Board from every walk of life and from every conceivable place. The leading veterans are now the leading citizens and predictably engaged in domestic and business pursuits far removed from the war. Some are prone to romanticizing their late experience:

> I would be very much pleased to learn that the Government was about to secure the Battle-field of Antietam for a National Park, preserving all the natural features that makes it interesting. I believe the field is comparatively unchanged since the war, and I know that I only express the feelings of the men of both sides in regards to a Battle-field where the gallantry displayed was creditable alike to each, and I should be still more pleased to have this plan perfected soon enough to allow the old soldiers of each army meet fraternally at a common Camp Fire on the old Battle Field, as a living example to our children that our differences are adjusted, our animosities wiped out and that we have but one common interest, one country and one flag.[26]

North and South alike, public and private citizens, government employees, politicians, lobbyists, journeymen, professionals, farmers; citizens all; they wrote, and they wrote with a clarity of thought and eloquence of expression that bequeaths to us a fleeting familiarity with and connection to the mindset of the Civil War survivor.

* * *

---

23 James Smith, letter to the Antietam Board, April 10, 1893, Carman Papers, Box 3, NYPL.

24 Jacob D. Cox, letter to General Henry Heth, Carman Papers, Box 3, NYPL.

25 W.H. Taylor, letter to the Antietam Board, Feb. 22, 1892, Carman Papers, Box 3, NYPL.

26 James Smith, letter to the Antietam Board.

Iron Antietam Battlefield Board tablets on the battlefield.
(Author)

Set on posts two feet off the ground and mounted at a 45-degree angle, the 3-foot by 4-foot cast iron tablets present their wordy faces to the reader like so many sunflowers to the sun.

There are hundreds of them spread over the battlefield, standing singly, in pairs, in groups of three, four and five, and in even larger series. Wherever they congregate, they signify, by the sheer weight of their numbers and presence. They have stood upon the field over 100 years, painted and repainted by successive park service crews, their words having been distilled and organized out of the accounts and memories of thousands of soldiers, their reversed impressions filled with molten metal in foundry sand, cast into raised words recounting the significant events that make for the sequence of events known as the Battle of Antietam.

To the contemporary visitor, the tablets are themselves remnants of history; the past that came into being after the battle. The commemorative past. The idea of history materialized into iron tablets.

Whether or not a park visitor comprehends the tablets with an active consciousness, they are hard to ignore. Their mere fact compels one to consider their origins and to compare their dense and specific narrative style with that of today's more generalized interpretive "stations."

While generalization provides narrative access, it hides layers of information and meaning. For every meaningful generalization, the tablets stand as a reminder of the differences in historical perception across time. The generalizations that allow the entire battle to be displayed in graphics and text on a single page tour map are valuable, and not to be dismissed interpretive windows. But between that map and these tablets there is a compelling story about how we see and remember.

* * *

Tablet No. 356, located on the west side of Rodman Avenue near its intersection with Burnside Bridge Road, reads:

> Jenkins' Brigade reached Sharpsburg at 11 A.M. September 15, and took position on the high ground west of the Cemetery. Late in the evening it moved to the high ground west of the Burnside Bridge Road, where it remained under artillery fire until 3 P.M. of the 17th, when it returned to its first position in support of Moody's and Squire's Batteries.
>
> It then advanced to the apple orchard and to the stone house and mill, about 250 yards north of this point, where it engaged the Federal line, which had reached this elevation. After the withdrawal of the enemy, the Brigade advanced its skirmishers over this ground to the crest of the hill overlooking the low ground and a belt of woodland bordering the Antietam. The Brigade was relieved by Fitzhugh Lee's Cavalry Brigade during the night of the 18th and at sunrise of the 19th crossed the Potomac at Blackford's Ford.[27]

Like all the other units engaged that day, the movements of Jenkins' Brigade were subject to the Antietam Board's scrutiny. Its validation process sought to ensure a reasonable accuracy in the narrative of a unit's action to be cast into a permanent iron tablet, and in the corresponding graphical representation of those movements in the developing battlefield atlas.

---

27 Large and Swisher, "Official History," 175-176.

Brigade commander Confederate Col. Joseph Walker's report in the *Official Records* reads in part:

> Here the brigade endured a terrific fire of shot and shell for some half hour, when, the ammunition of the artillery having been exhausted, it advanced some 400 yards to an apple orchard, under a heavy fire of artillery and small-arms. Perceiving the enemy in force in several positions, from any of which we were assailable, I threw out the First, Fifth, and Sixth Regiments South Carolina Volunteers to oppose him on the left, and the Palmetto Sharpshooters and the Second Regiment Rifles South Carolina Volunteers to meet him in the center and on the right. From this position we continued to pour a destructive fire into the ranks of the enemy, at short range, until he recoiled and retreated out of sight among the timber on Antietam Creek.[28]

The final tablet text hews closely to Walker's report. Where it differs is with its clarification and specificity as to which orchard Jenkins' Brigade advanced into; that is, the one associated with "the stone house and mill" as distinct from the Sherrick Farm. This point was no doubt resolved by Carman's exchange of letters with Walker in April of 1895 and with his subordinate, Capt. A.H. Foster of Company D of the Palmetto Sharpshooters.[29] Sending a small section of the base map then in use, Carman asked his correspondents to chart and describe the location and movement of their units. As he did in this case, Carmen then transcribed what information he deemed germane from the responses received onto his own uniform document system. Carman's task then became threefold: to reduce the most salient elements of the story into the space limitations of the proposed iron tablet, identify the appropriate location for the placement of the finished tablet on the field, and to transcribe the now verified narrative of movements onto the time phase maps of the *Atlas.* The editorial process required the utmost economy of expression.

---

28 *The War of the Rebellion: A Compilation of the Official Records of the Union and Confederate Armies* (Washington, DC: GPO, 1887), Series I, vol. 19, pt. 1, 905–908.
29 Ezra Ayers Carman, *Antietam Studies,* extracts from the National Archives, in the vertical files of the David Lilley Collection, Washington County Free Library, Western Maryland Room, Hagerstown, MD.

In the case instant, five days of action were reduced into 153 words to be cast by the Chattanooga foundry under contract to the War Department.[30]

While the tablet speaks to the orchard as being "about 250 yards north of this point," it is in fact due west of where the marker currently stakes its claim. Considering that the final placement of the tablets was constrained by the right of way strips of land that had been acquired for just these marking purposes, this directional differential is hardly surprising.

Ambiguity, while diminished, was not vanquished.

* * *

The work of the Antietam Board was intended to translate into permanent markers on the field. While the Board had begun by using temporary shingles stuck in the ground and nailed to trees, and had subsequently replaced those with less temporary wooden markers, by 1894 it had made no further progress. Sensing that the project lacked momentum, it was then that the War Department insisted that Colonel Stearns, who had only been able to work fitfully due to chronic illness, return to work. Unable to do so, he resigned, and it was then that Ezra Carman was appointed in his place as "historical expert."[31]

Equally as critical as the appointment of Carman at that time was that of George B. Davis as president. Davis was uniquely qualified for the post by virtue of his most recent assignment at the War Department where he had been overseeing the publication of the *Official Records of the War of the Rebellion.* Davis had also worked closely with Secretary of War Daniel S. Lamont on the development of departmental policy concerning the creation and maintenance of battlefield parks. It was Davis who had first articulated the "Antietam Plan" approach to battlefield park preservation. Rather than purchasing hundreds of contiguous acres, he advocated for strips of easements and rights of way, leaving the original properties in the hands of landowners. In this, Davis was a pragmatist, an attitude he brought to the Board's endeavors. He was committed to accomplishing its mission and possessed a realistic vision of the effort and resources needed to get it done.

---

30 In addition to Tablet No. 356, references to Jenkin's Brigade are found in three other tablets; No. 368 (Large and Swisher 45), No. 322 (Large and Swisher 46), and the continuation of No. 69 (Large and Swisher 172).

31 Snell and Brown, "Administrative History," 75-85.

Carman's role at Antietam was multifaceted, involving acquisition of "rights-of-way for the placement of the markers, for access roads through the battlefield, and for the purchase of land for the monument sites, including negotiation with landowners and the recording of deeds."[32] It was Carman and Davis who had the task of completing the organizing, synthesizing, and editing of the raw material gathered by the Antietam Board in the preceding years, Carman's encyclopedic knowledge informing the final product. In this respect the tablet narratives were a communal endeavor involving many hands, with particular credit being due to both Davis for driving the completion of the project and to Carman for originating much of the text involving Confederate troop movements and location.

It was a fruitful and productive collaboration. Between them, as this letter from President Davis indicates, they winnowed the raw material: "I have been engaged for several days in the preparation of drafts for tablets, and I will send them to you in packages, by Corps as soon as they have been completed. They are, as you may imagine, full of inaccuracies, the greater part of which will be removed by comparison and discussion."[33]

As important as the tablet narratives are, and as the most visible manifestation of the Antietam Board's work, much of Carman's fame stems from his lifelong endeavor to produce "a good map of the Antietam battle."[34] That a sound mapping system was crucial to the Board's work was very much understood by Davis. Using the Michler map as a base (which was prepared in 1867 by the topographic engineer and Brevet Brigadier General by the same name), three maps had been envisioned by Colonel Stearns and General Heth to tell the story of troop movements during the battle; the first "showing the position of the two Armies on the morning of September 17th before the battle began; the second showing the extreme advance of the Union forces during the

---

32 Scully, "Ezra Carman," 107.

33 Maj. George B. Davis, letter to Ezra Carman, Oct. 31, 1894, Antietam Battlefield Board papers, Series 706, Record Group 92, National Archives, quoted in Scully, "Ezra Carman," 110.

34 Carman's name is now paired with that of the supervising topographic engineer, Emmor Bradley Cope, the battle maps being generally referred to as the "Carman-Cope" maps. Col. Emmor Bradley Cope was the chief engineer of the Gettysburg Battlefield Commission who supervised the project, although most of the field work was done by his subordinates, Hays W. Mattern and Edgar M. Hewitt.

contest; the third showing the positions occupied by the contending armies after the battle terminated."[35]

Subsequently, and nearly simultaneous with his own appointment and that of Carman, Davis had seen to it that the Civil War's preeminent mapmaker Jed Hotchkiss was appointed as "expert topographer." In that selection Davis was to be disappointed. Hotchkiss was never able to meet Davis and Carman's requirements for a suitable base map, no matter how acceptable his efforts had been to Stonewall Jackson and the Confederate cause. Writing to the Secretary of War in 1895 prior to his departure, Davis expressed his frustration:

> The one thing awaiting to be done is to prepare a base map, and to locate upon it the positions of the troops at the different phases of the battle.
>
> My attempt to utilize Major Hotchkiss has well nigh proved a failure. He seemed to have just the qualities that were needed, not to make a survey of the field, but simply to correct the fence lines of the Michler map, (which was made in 1867, five years after the battle) and to bring out the precise topography of the field a little more clear than was done on that map.[36]

Both Carman and Davis believed they required a base map with a scale at least twice that of the Michler map in order to plot troop locations with sufficient accuracy.[37] Moreover, the concept of what would be sufficient to illustrate the movement of troops during the battle evolved over time so that by 1895, when the second Major Davis (George W.) had replaced the first Major Davis (George B.) as Board president, a succession of nine maps was envisioned. A year and a half later, Board President George W. Davis obtained the services of the engineers who had mapped

---

35 Antietam Board, report to Quartermaster General R.N. Batchelder, Jan. 13, 1894, Series 706, Record Group 92, National Archives, quoted in Snell and Brown, "Administrative History," 80.

36 Maj. George B. Davis, memorandum, Aug. 2, 1895, Series 706, Record Group 92, National Archives, quoted in Snell and Brown, "Administrative History," 100.

37 Davis memorandum of Aug. 2, 1895, quoted in Snell and Brown, "Administrative History," 100.

A plate from the Antietam Atlas (1908 edition) showing troop positions at 10:30 a.m. on Sept. 17, 1862. The scale of these maps can best be appreciated by knowing their size: 34" wide x 38" tall. (Library of Congress)

Gettysburg, and had a suitable Antietam base map completed by February 1898.[38]

Between then and the publication of the first edition of the completed atlas in 1904, Carman emerged as the principal and solitary figure laboring officially, and when the funding ran out, unofficially, to express

---

38 Trail, "Remembering Antietam," 230.

the product of the narrative tablet work as a map series. He continued to analyze and clarify the information that had been gathered for the tablets, and to receive and evaluate thousands of new pieces of information.

Ultimately consisting of 14 identical base maps, each one illustrating troop locations and movements in phases from "DAYBREAK" to "5.30 P.M.," the *Atlas of the Battlefield of Antietam* is the definitive representation of unit locations and movements. Forty-two years after Carman first conceived of the idea of a battle map of the engagement he had participated in and witnessed, 1,000 copies of the *Atlas* were struck and delivered to state libraries, GAR posts, and military units around the nation, as teaching devices, as jumping off points for further debate and discussion, and as historical resources for future generations.

What is unusual about the *Atlas* (and its Gettysburg twin) is its cartographic, information and design leap into graphic modernity. It abandons the hachure method of topographic illustration for the engineering precision of contour lines set at 10-foot intervals. The marking of fencing, roads, and fields under those lines, and the denoting of field cultivars with patterns of symbols, is an information layering technique characteristic of advanced graphic design. Overprinted on this are the modest and dispassionate thin red and blue bars of unit positions and lines, their identifying names produced in a wholly contemporary, block style, sans serif type. The overall result is so purely a visual information device that it is difficult to appreciate that it shares the same data foundation as the narrative content of the tablets themselves.

Although the feedback Carman received on the *Atlas* was largely an affirmation of his judgment and skill, it remained embedded with qualifiers that underscore the always tenuous business of exactitude.

From Edward S. Butts, President of The American National Bank of Vicksburg, Mississippi, March 6, 1905:

> Replying to your favor of February 24th, beg to say that I have received and examined the Atlas of Antietam, especially Plate 8. The position of Barksdale's Brigade on Plate 8 is correctly located, and subsequent positions are also approximately correct.[39]

---

39 Edward S. Butts, letter to Ezra Carman, March 6, 1905, Carman Papers, Box 3, NYPL.

From Gideon Spencer, Secretary and State Pension Agent, State Board
of Soldier's Relief, Providence, Rhode Island, March 15, 1905:

> The maps are spread upon my table and many of the
> members of old Battery D, 1st R.I. Light Artillery have
> examined it, and generally speaking, they agree as to the
> locations.[40]

In some instances, the commentary moved from expressions of general
agreement to explicit assertions of incorrectness, as in this comment from
John Lockhart, dated March 30, 1905:

> I examined the atlas thoroughly, and I find that you have
> placed the 69th P.V. in a supposed gap between the left
> and right flank of the 72nd P.V. and in front of same,
> which is entirely incorrect. There was no gap between our
> flanks, the 69th. was not there, for the reason that they
> were on the right of our regiment. It would be bad
> generalship in forming a brigade line of battle to place
> regiment in front of another. If the 69th. were where you
> placed it on the atlas, we could not have fired on the
> enemy until they had left our front.[41]

Over the next four years, Carman incorporated commentary like this
into his tactical understanding of the battle, producing a 1908 edition of
the *Atlas*, with 1,000 copies being ready for distribution in January 1909.

> There were approximately a dozen significant changes
> made in the information portrayed by the atlas. Among
> the most important were additions to the Confederate
> roster included with the set. In the first edition, only about
> one-third of the officers in command of Southern
> regiments were identified; by the 1908 revision, Carman
> had managed to learn the names of the commanders of

---

40 Gideon Spencer, letter to Ezra Carman, March 15, 1905, Carman Papers, Box #3,
NYPL.
41 John Lockhart, letter to Ezra Carman, March 30, 1905, Carman Papers, Box #3,
NYPL.

another one-third of the regiments. The remaining changes involved the maps. Some were accomplished simply by adding an arrow to show that a regiment either went a little further than previously shown, or took a slightly different route to its destination on the map, or perhaps suffered a reverse that had been neglected in the first edition.[42]

With Carman's death on Christmas day in 1909, the 1908 *Atlas* was the last chapter in the "official" version of Antietam.

* * *

The Congressional mandate required that the marking of the battlefield be accomplished "without praise and without censure."[43]

The language of qualitative action used on the tablets was thus damped down by a restrained and non-judgmental lexicon of: "engaged," "attacked," "overtook," "encountered," "advance," "deployed," "pursuit," "led," "secured," "fired into," "enfiladed," and "compelled to retire."

In defiance of this subdued vocabulary, the language of combat did ratchet up to: "raged," "sanguinary contest," "checked," "struck," "dislodged," "obstinate contest," "charge and counter charge of the most deadly character," and the penultimate expression of the tablets' narrative action: "maintained a contest rarely equaled in warfare."

This last phrase, describing the action of Wofford's brigade, Hood's division of Longstreet's command, tells of their advance from the Dunkard Church into the Miller Cornfield. Tablet No. 324 goes on to cite casualty numbers as a method of reinforcing the severity of the engagement:

> After losing more than one-half its numbers, the Brigade fell back to the fields southwest of the Dunkard Church, and was not again engaged. The Brigade went into action numbering 854; its loss in killed, wounded and missing

<hr>

42 David Lilley, "Genesis of the Carman-Cope Maps," 386.
43 Snell and Brown, "Administrative History," 98.

48

was 560. The 1st Texas carried into action 226 officers
and men, of whom 186 were killed or wounded."[44]

However worthy as vehicles for the transmission of a multiplicity of
facts and a now distant sensibility of language, the tablets are a difficult
gateway to understanding the battle.

Consider, for example, how bewildering the "order of battle" headers
at the top of each table are, and the redundancy inherent in organizing
the text around the military's chain of command.

Beginning with the obvious—Which army?—they drill down to the
corps or, in the Southern case, command level:

"Twelfth Army Corps
Maj. Gen. Jos. K.F. Mansfield, Commanding"[45]

And down further to the division:

"Williams' Division, Twelfth Army Corps
Brig. Gen. Alpheus S. Williams, Commanding"[46]

And then to the brigade, and the regiments composing it:

"Gordon's Brigade, Williams' Division
Brig. Gen. George H. Gordon, Commanding

Organization
2nd Massachusetts Infantry
3rd Wisconsin Infantry
27th Indiana Infantry
13th New Jersey Infantry
107th New York Infantry
Zouaves D'Afrique, Pennsylvania"[47]

What is conveyed on the corps or division level tablet in summary, is
often restated on a brigade level tablet in detail. Moreover, naming

---

44 Large and Swisher, "Battle of Antietam," 101-102. Tablet No. 324.
45 Large and Swisher, "Battle of Antietam," 72-73. Tablet No. 27.
46 Large and Swisher, "Battle of Antietam," 73. Tablet No. 28.
47 Large and Swisher, "Battle of Antietam," 73-74. Tablet No. 54.

conventions applied by both armies only add to the confusion; e.g., continuing to use the surnames of a unit's original commander even when, after having been killed or promoted, they were succeeded by another.

Relying solely on these tablets as a battlefield guide, one is likely to wander the 12-square-mile battlefield aimlessly in a hopeless tangle of information that only careful and prolonged study can sort out. It is the rare visitor who either wants or can sustain an appreciation on this level. Even supposing you know some larger things about the battle, the tablets can be enigmatic, their usefulness lost in the absence of a broader context. In their own way, they reinforce the axiom concerning small combat units; soldiers know no big thing, only that which they experience.

To some extent, the Antietam Board anticipated this need for a larger context, having placed "overview" tablets intended to give the reader a strategic sense of the battle and of its troop movements: the invasion of Maryland, the reduction of Harpers Ferry, and the battle of South Mountain. Their location at Bloody Lane assumed this to be the first stop for battlefield visitors (after perhaps dropping by the Cemetery superintendent's office). Visitors would then climb the observation tower at the end of the lane for the purpose of orienting themselves to the land.

The land was essential, of course, to appreciating the dimension and scope of the battle. It was also the common language shared by the survivors of the battle, the tableau to which they could return and which they could use to locate and describe their experience. It is the narrative thread that holds the tablet schema together. As an interpretive system it was sufficient so long as the primary audience was composed of survivors. They provided, as it were, their own interpretive context: foreknowledge of the land. The facts of mortality being what they are, however, and the ferrous structure of the tablets notwithstanding, the usefulness of this system as a meaningful guide to the battlefield diminished as quickly as it was erected. It was only as good as the living memory of the former soldiers.

Still, the tablet plan had been an intelligent solution to a significant interpretive problem. There had been an early plan to mark the lines of battle using poles topped with red and blue painted orbs, which would have resulted in a landscape of meaningless poles across a five-mile front, no organization of which could account for the small unit tactical considerations, the thrust, retreat and withdrawal of hundreds of units over the course of a long day. In concept, the pole idea was a graphic device, just too bound to its own tangible setting to be successful.

The narrative tablet approach closed the explanatory gap between the marker as the interpretive device and the locations it sought to represent by staking the explanations to the very ground near where the actions occurred, thus serving a double duty of giving geographic locus to the narrative event at the same time telling the story:[48]

" ... posted at and south of this point ..."

" ... it reached this point ..."

"... west of this ..."

"200 yards south of this ..."

That the result of these endeavors would age more quickly than their originators may have estimated underscores the always present risk of interpretive development. Our own milieu blinds us.

This transient condition of the marking system's interpretive relevance could not have escaped Carman or either one of the Major Davis's. All three were certainly touched by an historical consciousness even prior to their work at Antietam so that they were compelled to consider the problem; Carman as one of the founders of the New Jersey Historical Society and both Major Davis's through their work on the *Official Records*.[49] While focused on the tasks at hand, and having frequently discussed the marking system and its content, surely they engaged the question of how best to give overall coherence to their work at Antietam.

---

48 The narrative tablet approach was not unique to Antietam, having already been implemented at the battlefield site of Chickamauga. "It is proposed to use, for this purpose, tablets of cast iron, similar to those now furnished the Chickamauga Commission, by the Chattanooga Car and Foundry Company under its existing arrangement with the War Department. ... The same concern furnishes a cast iron guide board, which can be extensively used in marking the routes of corps." Maj. George B. Davis, report to Secretary of War Daniel S. Lamont, 7 Nov. 1894, Series 706, Record Group 92, National Archives; Snell and Brown, "Administrative History," 95.

49 On the biography of Maj. George B. Davis, see Snell and Brown, "Administrative History," 86; for that of Maj. George W. Davis, see Snell and Brown, "Administrative History," 101. The involvement of Maj. George W. Davis with the *Official Records* project is described in Trail, "Remembering Antietam," 220.

Just as surely that discussion must have continually come back to the *Atlas* which, in one form or another, had been under consideration since the formative days of the Antietam Board.[50]

As the surrogate graphical representation for the battlefield and the land, the *Atlas of the Battle of Antietam* achieved what the tablets could not: the symbolic display of troop movements over time. By filling this essential gap, the *Atlas* constitutes a framework for the tablet system. Any lack of cohesive understanding, or sense of the inadequacy of the tablets as interpretive devices, was salvaged by the manifestation of Ezra Carman's specific intelligence in the battlefield maps. Combined with the tablet system on the ground, the *Atlas* is the essential guide to the battle.

Touring the battlefield without the *Atlas* is like reading a text where all that remains are the footnotes to the now vanished narrative. Having preserved the tablet system in its entirety, one cannot suppose it to be a kind of apostasy for the National Park Service to have developed supplemental interpretive material over the years. But the general lack of availability of the *Atlas* is a major omission that ought to be corrected in order to restore the primacy and meaningfulness of the narrative tablet system.[51]

Thrusting cast iron forms of descriptive language into the soil where the unspeakable occurred is a good, even poetic thing, the earth itself providing the syntax for the disjointed and isolate stories on the tablets. We must say the thing, and saying it on the land where it happened, is as close as we can come to touching the event itself.

---

50 Although the appointment of Jed Hotchkiss had been a failure, and the Board was no closer to having a suitable base map at the end of 1895 than they had been four years prior, Carman and the first Maj. Davis continued to collaborate on what a map of the battle would look like. Their concept developed from the fairly static representation envisioned by the first Antietam Board, to the more dynamic series of maps that were finally produced. Carman had considered at one point what Maj. George B. Davis thought of as a significant graphical innovation, which was to "make the length of the rectangle, which represents a command on the map, form a fixed proportion of the strength of the command in battle," a technique that was abandoned due to the sheer volume of detail that had to be accommodated within the limited space of a map of any manageable scale. Maj. George B. Davis, memorandum, Aug. 2, 1895, quoted in Snell and Brown, "Administrative History," 100.

51 Although the text of the tablets is available in the book edited by George R. Large and Joe A. Swisher, there is no commercially available printed version of the *Atlas*, which is a significant interpretive omission. While electronic versions are available both on the internet (Library of Congress) and as a DVD, they are not a substitute for a field atlas. No doubt challenges of sizing have impeded that development.

But try as we might, we were not there. We do not carry the living memory of the soldiers who fought at Antietam nor are we able to. All we can do is strive for some approximation of their understanding, using as our means the tools they themselves left behind.

In Their Own Words: The Diary of Lieutenant James Simons, Bachman's (South Carolina) Battery, Army of Northern Virginia

by James A. Rosebrock

Between May 25, 1896, and February 1, 1905, James Simons wrote three letters to Ezra Carman about his experiences at the Battle of Antietam. In his first letter, Simons mentioned that he kept a diary that he had mislaid and promised "to hunt it up so as to verify my present recollection." In his second letter to Carman dated August 25, 1897, Simons attached an extract of the diary from September 14-19, 1862—the contents of which are enclosed in this article.[1]

James Simons Jr. was born on November 30, 1839, in Charleston, South Carolina. He was the son of James Simons, a former Speaker of the South Carolina House of Representatives and a militia general present at the firing on Fort Sumter. The younger Simons attended South Carolina College at Columbia and then the University of Leipzig in Germany. He was completing his law studies in August 1861 when William Bachman, a lawyer from Columbia who also attended college in Germany, began organizing Company H, "German Volunteers" of the Hampton Legion. Raised from the German community of Charleston, the company in November was converted to an artillery battery in the Legion and became an independent artillery company in June 1862. Equipped with two 12-lb Napoleons and two 12-lb Blakely rifles, the battery was assigned to the artillery battalion of Brig. Gen. John Bell Hood's division commanded by Maj. Bushrod W. Frobel. At Antietam, First Lieutenant Simons commanded the Napoleon section of his battery.[2]

---

1 James Simons to Ezra Carman, May 25, 1896, August 25, 1897, and February 1, 1905, National Archives-Antietam Studies.

2 James A. Rosebrock, *The Artillery of Antietam*, (Sharpsburg MD: Antietam Institute Press, 2023), 247.

On September 14, 1862, Hood's division marched from Hagerstown to Boonsboro to reinforce Maj. Gen. D.H. Hill's beleaguered division defending the South Mountain passes. Our story begins there.

BEGINNING OF DIARY

SEPTEMBER 14th SUNDAY

About 9:00 o'clock A.M. we were put in motion - about 4 o'clock in the afternoon we passed through the town of Boonsboro, and the terror stricken and anxious appearance

James Simons
(Find a Grave)

of the townspeople showed that trouble was ahead - we had got but a short distance out of the town before the discharges of artillery and the rattle of musketry told us of bloody work before us - the roads were filled with citizens flying from the battlefield, and the scenes of strife, now and terrible to them, but familiar to us, who had for many months had the horrors of war for an everyday sight. Gen. Garland had been fighting the enemy here for some time previous to our arrival the battle took place just at Boonsboro gap and the mountain rose like walls on either side of us.[3] Our battery was posted in a small field just on the other side of the road, from the house where the ladies had waved confederate flags to us as we passed on our way to Hagerstown - About 100 yards in front of our battery there was a thick woods, and patiently did we wait under a hailstorm of minie bullets for the enemy to emerge to pour into them a volley of canister - On our left just before the mouth of the gap there was a line of our Infantry, which was very much exposed, with shot and shell ploughing the ground on every side of them - I saw one shell burst exactly in the line carrying death and destruction to many a brave one - Just by our battery was Gen. Longstreet with whose appearance and behavior I was very much struck - He wore a pair of slippers and sat on his horse reading a paper, his countenance entirely unmoved by the scene of terror which was being enacted all around him. A shrapnel burst in a tree just in front of him raining down its fragment all around him, but he did not

---

3 Brigadier General Samuel Garland Jr. (1830-1882) commanded a brigade in Maj. Gen. D.H. Hill's division and was killed at Fox's Gap on September 14, 1862.

even raise his eyes from his paper, but read on with an air of utter concern. The minie balls which sung around us in profusion like a swarm of mosquitoes in one of the low lots in Charleston in the summer time had no effect upon him. We remained here until dark and we could scarcely see fifty yards in front of us, and expecting the shower of minie balls, which had fallen incessantly without intermission to be succeeded by a charge, when our line on our left after fighting gallantly were overpowered by numbers and fell back beyond our battery. Still, we moved not, but remained inactively although the peril of the battery was imminent, and I expected every moment in the darkness to have the foe spring upon us. Finally, Gen. Evans cried to us to retire the battery without delay, else it was lost.[4] We got out safely this time. Our troops although driven back on the left, held the gap when darkness put an end to the fight. We've bivouacked in a field on the left of the road going to the town about a quarter of a mile from the gap. We had hardly laid down to snatch a short repose before we were awakened and received orders to march. We marched through Boonsboro and took a road to the left leading to Sharpsburg. This was a retrograde movement, but it did not surprise or depress us as we knew that a large portion of our army had marched against Harpers Ferry and that our able commanding General could only have desired to hold the enemy, who was in full force, in check here, so as to give the rest of the army time to make a junction with him at some point in the vicinity of Sharpsburg. And in this he was entirely successful, as at dark when the fight necessarily ceased, we held the gap and could during the night fall back and make a junction with the rest of the army. We marched the whole enduring night, overcome and worn out by exhaustion and fatigue. I frequently fell asleep on my horse and would awake by finding myself nearly falling off. During the night I met a cavalry officer who told me that during a skirmish which took place in the streets of Frederick a few days ago between some of Gen. Hampton's and some of the Federal cavalry Gen. Hampton have been shot at by several of the civilians.

---

4 Brigadier General Nathan "Shanks" Evans (1824-1868) commanded an independent brigade of South Carolina troops at the Battle of Antietam.

SEPTEMBER 15th MONDAY

Just before daylight we passed through Keedysville a small town and our division being rearguard, we formed a line of battle on the heights about a mile beyond the town. Here we remained about half hour after which we resumed the march. About 12 o'clock M. we crossed the Antietam and came up with the rest of the army at Sharpsburg. Our battery immediately took position on the right of the main road looking towards the enemy, in a cornfield. We had not been here an hour before heavy clouds of dust heralded the approach of the enemy. Shortly after the dark columns of the blue coats were seen advancing preceded by a cloud of skirmishers. They came up cautiously, and made their arrangements for the attack with the greatest deliberation. Meanwhile on every side, everyone was asking his neighbor have you seen where Jackson is or how long will it take Jackson to come from Harpers Ferry and many were the speculations indulged in as to whether we would have to fight the immense force opposed to a single handed and alone - or weather Jackson would come up in time to share the danger. In a very short time, the enemy got several batteries in the position, and an artillery duel was commenced. Very few of our batteries were allowed to fire, while most were ordered to retain their fire for the infantry. Among the latter number we were, and we patiently had to submit and endure, while each shot the enemy fired at us was better than the last. It is extraordinary how much better they shoot when their fire is not returned. I have tried them both ways and speak from experience.[5]

SEPTEMBER 16th TUESDAY

We all expected the battle to open with the day, but were agreeably surprised to find the enemy did not advance as we well knew that every hour brought Gen. Jackson and reinforcements nearer. As the day advanced the enemy opened on our position with his batteries. Very little artillery was permitted to reply. We again had patiently to submit, and as they by this time had elegant range of us, we found it pretty hot. Every

---

5 Though assigned to Hood's division, Frobel's artillery batteries were positioned just east of Sharpsburg and covering the Middle Bridge and Boonsboro Pike. They did not support Hood's division during the battle.

now and then they would open up on us with terrible fury and keep it up sometimes for an hour and then cease firing when there would be a complete lull in the storm. At times the fire was awfully severe the air being completely alive with the shrieking and bursting monsters. We had only one man wounded priv. [Henry] Hinck in the hand severely, and one horse shot in the shoulder and disabled.[6] There was a little ridge by our battery behind which they sought protection during the fire which we were not allowed to return. Behind this the greater portion of our company was huddled together with a great many of the infantry. I saw a large rifle shell almost as long as my fore arm strike the ridge and grazing another man, nestle quietly against the leg of Robert Rutledge who happened at the time to be there too. There was a second of the most awful suspense everyone expecting it to burst and as we were very crowded hardly one could have escaped. Fortunately, however it did not explode and to avoid against accidents it was carefully carried some distance from the party. I saw a shell strike just behind us among the infantry supports and bursting literally tear a man to atoms scattering pieces of him and his accoutrements in every direction. It was very tantalizing to have to abstain from returning the fire. We could see the "federal" Artillerist at their guns, and when they ceased firing, we could see them all go under the shade of a large tree where they would remain until ordered to open again. During the day I frequently saw Gens. Lee and Longstreet. During our stay here we had the pleasure of the society of Colonel P. F. Stevens, whose brigade was supporting our battery.[7] As night came on, I spread my blanket which I carry on my saddle and sharing it with Capt. Bachman retired to rest.

SEPTEMBER 17th. WEDNESDAY

At Six o'clock the sharp crack of the skirmisher's rifles, immediately followed by the roar of the artillery announced that the battle of Sharpsburg or as the "federals" call it the battle of Antietam had begun. This proved to be the severest battle of the war and lasted without

---

6 U.S. Compiled Service Records of Confederate Soldiers Who Served in Organizations from the State of South Carolina 1861-1865, National Archives.

7 At the start of the Maryland Campaign Brig. Gen. Nathan Evans had command of a temporary division consisting of Brig. John B. Hood's brigades and his own independent brigade, and he assigned his senior colonel Peter F. Stevens (1830-1910) the commander of the Holcombe Legion to command the brigade.

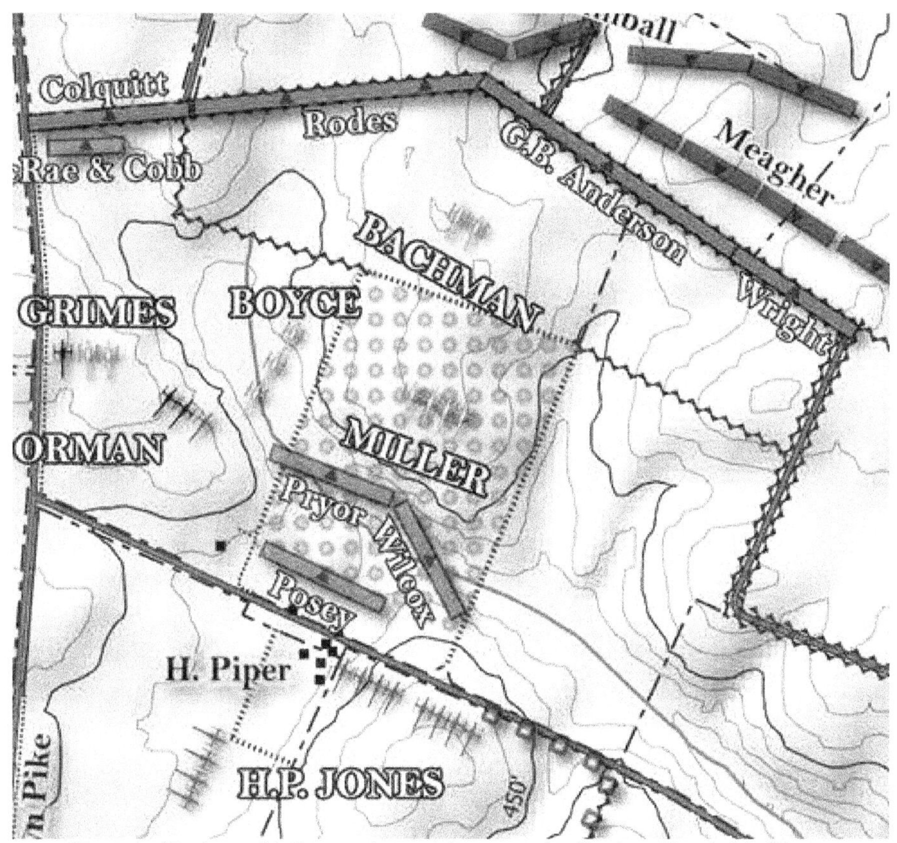

Simon's (Bachman's) Battery in position near the Sunken Road, 10: 30 a.m.
(Aaron Holley)

interruption until 7 P.M. The ground was very open and very well adapted for the use of artillery, and battery upon battery was engaged. From one side of the field to the other, the whole air was filled with artillery projectiles appearing to come from every direction. We remained in the same position we had occupied hitherto until about 10 o'clock A.M. when the two napoleon guns were ordered to the left. We passed through a most awful fire to get there, and reported to Gen. Longstreet who was again [on] the field in his slippers, riding with Gen. Lee. They both appeared entirely unmoved. He ordered us still further to the left. At this time everybody was in the greatest anxiety for the arrival of Gen. Jackson, who was absent not only with his corps d'Armee, but with several divisions of ours (Gen. Longstreet)—It was with feeling of infinite relief that we heard that he was coming on and not far off. Gen. Anderson's division soon appeared and went in near us. Maj. Gen. D. H.

Hill now conducted our section to a very exposed position, not more than one hundred and fifty yards from the enemy's line of battle. We could see them plainly. We saw just in front of us two United States flags and one blue one. So near were we, that we could almost count the stars on their flags. We promptly opened on them with canister, ploughing up their line all around their flags. a Hail storm of minie balls commenced to rain on us, not to speak of shell and solid shot, which tore up the very ground on which we were. We continued, however with our canister. But the sharp shooters of the enemy swarmed in a woods, very little more than fifty yards from our left, and behind the trees of which they sheltered themselves. From behind their cover, they poured into us a galling fire and soon they disabled six horses out of the twelve in the two pieces (the caissons having been left in a more secure place). The horses did not fall immediately, and we were able to draw off a little to the rear. The horse which had been disabled yesterday hobbled after us when we went into this position and was killed by a rifle ball. Sergt J. C. Hahn and private [Fritz Kassler] Kessler were both pierced through the abdomen with many bullets, and private [Henry] Hollings had one to pass through his haversack rations, tin plate, and through both thighs inflicting a very painful and severe wound.[8] Our gun carriages and handspikes have still minie bullets embedded in them. Our men on the right began to give way. Reduced by fatigue, sufferings, exhaustion, and disease ours, in the beginning small force, became terribly diminished by straggling, which took place to an alarming extent although those who remained fought like tigers, the enemy drove them back on the right into the very town of Sharpsburg but were received by our Artillery with a sheet of fire. Just at this time Gen. Chilton A. G. to General Lee ordered us up to the right on the hills just in rear of Sharpsburg and we reached there just in time to see the enemy hurled back.[9] It was now about 5 o'clock P.M. and the division of the gallant Major General A. P. Hill of Gen. Jackson's Corps going in on the right with the cheer, followed up the successes of the Artillery, and reinstated our line in its original position. It is impossible to give a faint idea of the horrors of this battle which lasted thirteen hours without intermission. Every part of the field was covered with dead and wounded, and now and then the din of battle would be swallowed up in

---

8 U.S. Compiled Service Records of Confederate Soldiers Who Served in Organizations from the State of South Carolina 1861-1865, National Archives.
9 Lieutenant Colonel Robert H. Chilton (1815-1879) served as an adjutant general on Lee's staff during the Maryland Campaign.

the report of the explosion of a caisson. Providence was again with our Company and our loss was very small compared with the dangers through which we passed. I escaped very narrowly - a piece of shell struck my sabre, and while I was pointing one of the napoleons, a minie ball buried itself in the cheek of the gun carriage within a few inches of my head and another in the trail just barely grazing my leg. At dark we went to the rear and bivouacked in a large field near our division hospital. I omitted to mention, that while we were going into position where we fired on the enemy with canister, we passed through a superb apple orchard and in spite of shells, shot and minie balls our boys could not be restrained from bagging the apples which by the by were very fine. As soon as we got into bivouac Capt. B. and myself went over to the hospital to see our suffering comrades. Here we found doctor Buist attending them with the greatest tenderness.[10] Our poor friends bore their sufferings heroically, but we soon saw that poor Hahn and Kassler had but a short time to live. The hospital was in a large orchard and the whole ground was strewn with mangled sufferers. We saw here Lieut. [Samuel] Pringle[11] of Capt. Garden's Battery, who had lost his leg by a Cannon ball. He was suffering intensely. Just as he was wounded, his battery retired, and with difficulty he was carried and secreted in the basement of one of the houses, on the edge of the town while the fighting raged fiercely all around him. When the enemy was driven back, he was brought to the rear having suffered severely. Near our bivouac we met our old friends Col. S. D. Lee and Capt. Moody.[12]

SEPTEMBER 18th. THURSDAY

We expected the enemy to renew the attack today, but they were evidently too badly crippled. I learned with great regret that Major Dingle of the Hampton Legion and other of our friends had been killed.[13] I rode

---

10 Assistant Surgeon John S. Buist (1839-1910) served with Frobel's artillery battalion at Antietam. Frobel commended Buist in his report "for his attention to the sick."
11 Lieutenant Samuel M. Pringle (1839-1862) commanded a section of guns in Capt. Hugh Garden's Palmetto Battery, also assigned to Frobel's battalion. He died of his wounds on September 24, 1862.
12 Colonel Stephen D. Lee (1833-1908) commanded one of the Reserve artillery battalions at Antietam. Captain George V. Moody (1816-1866) commanded the Madison (Louisiana) Battery, and was one of Lee's commanders.
13 Major James H. Dingle (1824-1862) served as a major in the Hampton Legion and was killed in action at Sharpsburg.

over a portion of the field, passing through the town of Sharpsburg. I saw several houses burned down, and all were more or less torn and shattered by shot and shell while many dead bodies and horses were lying in the streets. I went as far as the position our battery had first occupied when we came to this place. We certainly whipped the enemy, on the right and left and held our own in the center. The best proof of the result of the contest is that the enemy did not renew the attack. About Mid-day we crossed the Potomac and bivouacked on the soil of Virginia near Shepherdstown in a pouring rain. In the evening, I met my friend Major Venable of Gen. Lee's staff, who told me that the impression that we had gained a victory was entirely correct.[14] We heard the particulars of the capture of Harpers Ferry filled with stores and munitions of war of the best description.

SEPTEMBER 19th. FRIDAY

Last night our whole army crossed the Potomac and the enemy commenced to shell us with their long-range guns, our battery replying. We started to march about 10 o'clock A.M. and marched to Halltown, where we arrived about dark and halted for a short time. We continued the march, passed through Charles Town, a mile beyond which we bivouacked about 11 o'clock P.M.

END OF DIARY

Simon's diary provides us with a valuable first-person contemporaneous account of the actions of an artillery lieutenant commanding a section of guns in the Bloody Lane. We encounter Lee and Longstreet at various times and meet several of Lee's staff officers actively involved in the placing of artillery at Antietam. Simons brings the battle to a personal and violent level recounting the scenes of the battle afterward and the terrible suffering of his comrades in arms Samuel Pringle, J.C. Hahn and Fritz Kassler.

James Simons survived the war and became a successful lawyer in Charleston practicing law with his father until the latter's death in 1879 whereupon he established his own law firm. In 1878 Simons was elected

---

14 Major Charles S. Venable (1827-1900) served as an aide de camp to General Lee during the Maryland Campaign.

to the South Carolina House of Representatives, serving as speaker of the House from 1882-1890. He was prominent in Charleston business and cultural affairs serving as president of the South Carolina State Society of the Cincinnati. He died on July 4, 1919, at the age of 79.[15]

15 James Simons personal papers, 1875-1919, South Carolina Historical Society.

Antietam Artifacts: The Sword of Wilson Colwell, 2nd Wisconsin Infantry
by Brian Wyland

The assistant surgeon approached the seated captain commanding the skirmish line near Turner's Gap and asked if he was wounded. "Yes, and I fear badly," was the reply. "Go tell the boys to advance the right and press forward—not give way." Upon fulfilling the order, the assistant surgeon returned and asked what he could do for the soldier. "Get a couple of the boys to take me back behind our battery as I don't want to fall into the hands of the enemy." It was during the execution of this request that the captain exclaimed, "My poor, poor wife," and passed from this earth. Colonel Lucius Fairchild of the 2nd Wisconsin captured this episode in the closing sentences of his after-action report for the September 14, 1862, Battle of South Mountain[1]:

> Captain Colwell, of Company B, was killed while in command of the line of skirmishers. His place can hardly be filled. He was a fine officer and beloved by the whole regiment.[2]

Wilson Colwell was born in Kittanning, Pennsylvania, on April 13, 1827, the son of Alexander and Margaret Colwell. After attending Jefferson College in Canonsburg, Pennsylvania, he entered the iron business, first with his wealthy father and then on his own. By 1858, Colwell had moved to western Wisconsin to the city of La Crosse where he founded a bank. It was during his time in Wisconsin that he married Nannie Hammer, on May 19, 1858, and the couple welcomed the birth of their first child, also named Nannie, in February of 1859. Colwell

---

1 Frank Hatch to Indiscernible, September 23, 1862, Catalog of Articles Surrounding the Death of Captain Wilson Colwell, September 14, 1862, MISC MSS 147, La Crosse Public Library Archives, La Crosse, WI.
2 *War of the Rebellion: The Official Records of the Union and Confederate Armies* (Washington, DC: GPO, 1887), Series 1, vol. 19, pt. 1, 253. Hereafter cited as *OR,* all citations from Series 1 unless otherwise stated.

Wilson Colwell, 2nd Wisconsin Infantry.
(Wisconsin Historical Society, WHI-69931)

became captain of the local militia unit, the La Crosse Light Guard, and was elected the city's mayor in the spring of 1861. He served as mayor for only a short time before enlisting as a soldier, following the firing on Fort Sumter and the onset of the United States Civil War. Captain Colwell and the Light Guard tendered their service to the state on April 18, 1861, and after training at Camp Randall in Madison, the unit mustered into United States service on June 11 for the term of three years as Company B of the 2nd Wisconsin Infantry.[3]

Colwell's physical appearance was described as imposing and inspiring:

> His frame was tall, fully developed in every limb, and strongly built. His features massive and wearing in repose an expression almost of sternness and austerity; but his genial humor and kindly nature were easily appealed to, and his ordinary expression was one peculiarly pleasing and attractive. A full beard and black hair of silky fineness and lustre, worn long, gave him a marked and distinguished appearance in civil life, and on the field of battle an air of superiority and command.[4]

His personality and leadership characteristics also garnered praise and respect:

> His kindness and generosity, with a pleasant humor, often veiled under an affected gruffness, caused the men to regard him with a positive feeling of affection, and this in his company, to a great extent, supplied the place of discipline. He was incapable by nature of enduring or enforcing a martinet discipline; but the men knew him so well, and were so strongly attached to him that he easily

---

3 E. B. Quiner, "Regimental History—Second Infantry," in *Military History of Wisconsin* (Chicago: Clarke & Co., Publishers, 1866),438, Retrieved from https://content.wisconsinhistory.org/digital/collection/quiner/id/16283/rec/4; "The Old Iron Brigade," *Milwaukee Sunday Telegraph,* September 23, 1883, 2, Catalog of Articles Surrounding the Death of Captain Wilson Colwell, September 14, 1862, MISC MSS 147, La Crosse Public Library Archives, La Crosse, WI; *Soldiers' and Citizens' Album of Biographical Record Containing Personal Sketches of Army Men and Citizens Prominent in Loyalty to the Union: Also a Chronological and Statistical History of the Civil War* (Chicago: Grand Army Publishing Company, 1890), 762.
4 "The Old Iron Brigade," 2.

maintained a perfect discipline when necessity called for it.[5]

The 2nd Wisconsin left Madison for Washington, DC, by train on June 20 and reached the nation's capital on June 25 where it was assigned to Col. William Tecumseh Sherman's brigade in Brig. Gen. Daniel Tyler's division. By July 18, Colwell and his company were in the vicinity of the fighting near Blackburn's Ford in Virginia, and three days later participated in one of the failed assaults up Henry Hill during the First Battle of Manassas. An episode from these early actions of the war helps explain the admiration and attraction soldiers had toward Capt. Colwell. During the fighting near Blackburn's Ford, a soldier of Company B was mortally wounded when hit in the leg by a solid shot. As the artillery projectiles continued to land amongst the men, Colwell sat down to smoke his pipe on the very spot where the mortal wounding had occurred. He justified his decision to those around him, commenting that "lightning never strikes twice in the same place."[6]

In September of 1861, the 2nd Wisconsin constructed fortifications and performed picket duty near Chain Bridge in Northern Virginia and in early October was brigaded with the 6th Wisconsin, 7th Wisconsin, and 19th Indiana under the command of Brig. Gen. Rufus King. With the advancement of King to lead a division in the spring of 1862, leadership of the brigade eventually transferred to Brig. Gen. John Gibbon in May. The 2nd Wisconsin engaged in skirmishing actions in July and August of 1862 and participated in heavy fighting near the Brawner Farm on the evening of August 28 as they fought the command of Maj. Gen. Thomas Jackson, opening the Second Battle of Manassas. As the multi-day battle continued, the regiment served in a supporting role on August 29 and then acted as the rear guard, with the rest of the brigade, on August 30 as the Union army retreated from the field.[7]

Deciding the best course of action was to move into Northern territory, Gen. Robert E. Lee and the Army of Northern Virginia began its push into Maryland in early September of 1862. As Gen. George B. McClellan

---

5 Ibid.

6 Quiner, *Military History of Wisconsin*, 438-440; George H. Otis, *The Second Wisconsin Infantry*, ed., Alan D. Gaff (Dayton, OH: Morningside House, Inc., 1984), 61.

7 Quiner, *Military History of Wisconsin*, 442-446, 448; Otis, *The Second Wisconsin Infantry*, 48, 52-55, 57-58.

and the Army of the Potomac pursued, Colwell and the 2nd Wisconsin marched to Washington, DC, and then through Maryland where they eventually came to the base of South Mountain in the early afternoon of September 14. As battle raged on to their right and left, Gibbon's regiments remained unengaged until around 5:00 p.m. when they were ordered to move up the National Road and assault Turner's Gap. Companies B and E of the 2nd Wisconsin, selected as skirmishers and led by Captain Colwell, were ordered to rest their right on the road as they ascended South Mountain.[8]

Followed by the 19th Indiana and the 2nd Wisconsin, and with the 7th and 6th Wisconsin to their right preceded by skirmishers from the latter regiment, Colwell and his command pushed up the slope toward Turner's Gap where they would confront Confederates in the brigade of Col. Alfred H. Colquitt. During this assault, Colwell received mortal wounds in the lower abdomen from enemy musket fire and died on South Mountain. His body was transferred to Washington, DC, and eventually back to his birthplace of Kittanning for burial. The soldier tasked with transporting Colwell's remains also brought with him the captain's sword, which in time was passed to his wife. The sword remained in the family until it was donated to the La Crosse County Historical Society in 1965 where it continues to be housed and cared for today.[9]

The sword is a Model 1850 Foot Officer's and is approximately 36 inches in length. The sword's hilt's pommel and guard are brass gilded, and the grip is wrapped with brass wire. The blade, which is slightly curved, measures about 30 inches in length with a width in the middle of about one inch. Etched along both sides of the blade is a foliage motif, and one side also appears to include an etching of an eagle design similar to that of the Great Seal of the United States. Within the etchings on the other side are the letters "US" as well as markings indicating that the

---

8 Otis, *The Second Wisconsin Infantry*, 59- 60; *OR,* vol. 19, pt.1, 144, 170, 249, 252.
9 Norman Eastman to M.M. Pomeroy, September 17, 1862, *La Crosse Weekly Democrat,* September 23, 1862; "The Old Iron Brigade," 2; *OR,* vol. 19, pt.1, 247; Terence Boschert, "Colwell – Dorset Auction to Bring End to an Era," *La Crosse Sunday Tribune,* October 17, 1965.

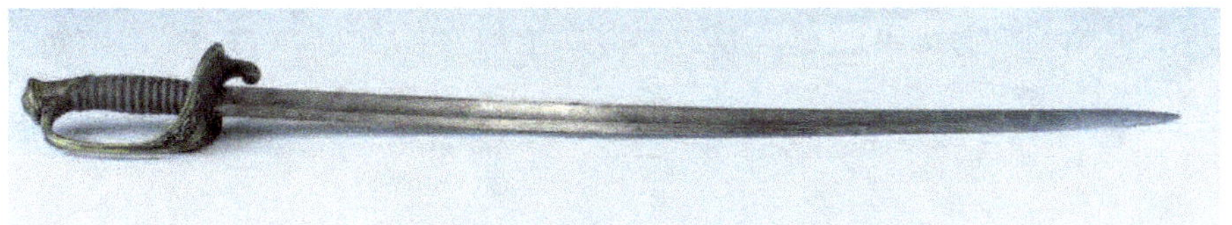

Wilson Colwell's Sword. (La Crosse County Historical Society)

Ames Manufacturing Company of Chicopee, Massachusetts, produced the sword.

Despite his death, Wilson Colwell's courage and influence continued to be honored by those who knew and served with him. A poem about the captain titled "The Tobacco Pipe," is part of the regimental history of the 2nd Wisconsin and Wilson Colwell Post 38 of the Grand Army of the Republic was organized in La Crosse during July of 1882. The excerpt below from a Civil War veteran reunion article succinctly captures Colwell's service and sacrifice during his time in the army[10]:

> The only son of wealthy parents, reared in luxury, accustomed to the gratification of every wish, and the unbroken enjoyment of every comfort, he passed through all the annoyances and discomforts of camp and march without a murmur. From the day of his enlistment to the hour of his glorious death, he stood the ideal of a patriot citizen in arms, ready, eager, and capable to endure any hardship or fatigue, to dare any danger and suffer any death which his country could require of him.[11]

Although not one of the more well-known individuals who fought at South Mountain, Wilson Colwell's story—like all stories of the soldiers and citizens whose lives were impacted by the Maryland Campaign of 1862—deserves to be told, appreciated, and remembered.

I would like to give my sincere appreciation and thanks to Amy Vach of the La Crosse County Historical Society whose assistance and insight contributed significantly towards the writing of this article. I would also like to express my gratitude to Laura Marfut of the Antietam Institute for

---

10 "Large Room in Court House Basement Recalls Memories of Meetings of Civil War Veterans," *La Crosse Tribune and Leader-Press,* November 2, 1941, 7; Otis, *The Second Wisconsin Infantry,* 61- 62.

11 "The Old Iron Brigade," 2.

*her suggestion to explore writing an article for the Antietam Journal.—
Brian Wyland*

In Antietam's Footsteps: The September 1862 Harpers Ferry Battlefield
by J. O. Smith

The largest Civil War battle in what is now West Virginia and the signature Confederate success in the Maryland Campaign of 1862 culminated on the morning of September 15, 1862, at Harpers Ferry. Nearly 13,000 Federal soldiers, hemmed in from three directions, surrendered to a Confederate force under "Stonewall" Jackson that had set out from Frederick five days earlier to eliminate the threat posed by the Federal garrison at Harpers Ferry. Preservation efforts in recent decades have saved much of this hallowed ground, allowing the battlefield tramper to appreciate the perspectives from both sides of the line and understand a critical part of the campaign.

Just outside of the historic town are two ridgelines where the battle concluded—Bolivar Heights and Schoolhouse Ridge. After leaving Loudoun Heights undefended and losing Maryland Heights on September 13, Federal forces controlled only one approach into Harpers Ferry—the Charlestown Pike (Route 340). Three Confederate divisions closed in from the west along the pike. The National Park Service provides convenient access to both the Union position on Bolivar Heights and the Confederate position on Schoolhouse Ridge. At Bolivar Heights, a trail circles a portion of the Federal defenses and branches down to the skirmish line. Crossing Bakerton Road, the visitor can ascend Schoolhouse Ridge to gain a view from the Confederate perspective. Across Route 340 from the Bolivar Heights parking lot is the Murphy Farm (known as the Chambers Farm in 1862), where guns mark the Confederate position that enfiladed the Union line on Bolivar Heights as A. P. Hill's division closed the trap on Harpers Ferry.[1]

The Bolivar Heights lot is near what was the center of the Federal line north of the Charlestown Pike. Though trees obscure much of the westward view today, an opening provides a glimpse of Schoolhouse Ridge and Confederate artillery pieces just under a mile away. In the opposite direction, Maryland Heights and Loudoun Heights loom over the town to the east and the Federal position. Bolivar Heights rises about

---

1 Dennis E. Frye, *Antietam Revealed: The Battle of Antietam and the Maryland Campaign as You Have Never Seen It Before* (Collingswood, NJ: C. W. Historicals, LLC, 2004), 21.

300 feet above the valley floor, far below Maryland Heights and Loudoun Heights, but 200 feet higher than the Confederate position on Schoolhouse Ridge. At midafternoon on September 14, Confederate artillery opened on Union troops from three directions—Schoolhouse Ridge to the west, Loudoun Heights to the southeast, and Maryland Heights to the northeast. A 9th Vermont captain remembered the soldiers moving back and forth across the heights to try to escape the bombardment: "Whichever slope we were on, we wished it were the other one." A soldier in the newly mustered 125th New York remarked that "it is dreadful to be a mark for artillery, bad enough for any but especially for raw troops." Although Federal casualties were light, the shelling demoralized the Harpers Ferry defenders, including, as it turned out, the Federal high command.[2]

Near the Bolivar Heights lot, a trail descends the slope through the trees in the direction of Schoolhouse Ridge, first passing through the Union picket line, as told by a series of waysides. Across Bakerton Road, a trail climbs Schoolhouse Ridge to the Confederate line, which affords a panorama of the imposing Union position on Bolivar Heights. A Confederate infantry assault would have required an advance across several hundred yards of open fields before an ascent to the high ground where Federal infantry would have been waiting. From Schoolhouse Ridge, there also is a clear view of natural swales cut in the Bolivar Heights ridgeline that provided defilade to Union soldiers trying to withstand the Confederate artillery barrage. With Loudoun Heights in the distance on the right and Maryland Heights on the left, the visitor also can appreciate Jackson's challenges in coordinating his converging forces, with rivers and ridges separating all three.[3]

Rather than order what likely would have been a costly frontal assault across the open ground between Schoolhouse Ridge and Bolivar Heights, Jackson moved A. P. Hill's division to his right on the evening of September 14. At the Chambers-Murphy farm, a walk along the bluff overlooking the Shenandoah River illuminates the accomplishments of A. P. Hill's men to position themselves on the flank of the Bolivar

---

2 Frye, *Antietam Revealed*, 32-33; D Scott Hartwig, *To Antietam Creek: The Maryland Campaign of September 1862* (Baltimore: The Johns Hopkins University Press, 2012), 533; Frye, "Drama between the Rivers: Harpers Ferry in the 1862 Maryland Campaign," in *Antietam: Essays on the 1862 Maryland Campaign*, Gary W. Gallagher, ed. (Kent, OH: The Kent State University Press, 1989), 27.

3 Hartwig, *To Antietam Creek*, 529-530.

The Confederate gun line on Schoolhouse Ridge can be visited today at Harpers Ferry National Historical Park. Bolivar Heights is the wooded ridge in the center of the photograph. Maryland Heights can be seen above Bolivar Heights to the left and Loudoun Heights towers above Bolivar Heights to the right. (Kevin R. Pawlak)

Heights line. Two of Hill's brigades marched along the railroad next to the Shenandoah River and climbed its "precipitous banks" to get into position. One of Hill's South Carolinians could not understand why they were "allowed to climb the precipitous height." As he saw it, "[a] handful of the enemy could have beaten back an army here, for it was so steep that a man could hardly carry his arms up it." When morning arrived on September 15, Confederate batteries on the farm constituted part of the approximately 60 Confederate guns laying down a ring of fire from Schoolhouse Ridge, Loudoun Heights and Maryland Heights. Surrounded, its supply of artillery rounds depleted, and holding little hope of relief, the Federal garrison at Harpers Ferry did not prolong the matter and surrendered between 8 and 9 a.m. Jackson's men had accomplished their objective. Lee's campaign north of the Potomac could continue, as the victorious Confederates now set out for the heights of Sharpsburg along Antietam Creek.[4]

The Bolivar Heights parking lot is off of Rte. 340 at the end of Whitman Ave. N 39.32374, W 77.76115. The Murphy/Chambers Farm is nearby at the intersection of Campground Road and Old Taylor Lane. N 39.31250, W 77.76116.

4 Hartwig, *To Antietam Creek*, 533-534, 556; James Fitz James Caldwell, *The History of a Brigade of South Carolinians, Known First as "Gregg's" and Subsequently as "McGowan's Brigade* (Philadelphia: King & Baird, Printers, 1866), 43; Frye, "Drama Between the Rivers," 33.

Institute Interview: Sitting Down with Dennis Frye
by Laura L. Marfut

Dennis Frye retired in 2018 after 32 years with the National Park Service at Harpers Ferry National Historical Park, 20 of those years as Chief Historian. He has published 11 books and written hundreds of articles. His name is synonymous with Harpers Ferry as a Civil War historic site.

Dennis is the recipient of many prestigious awards, including the National Book of the Year Award from the Association of Partners for Public Lands for his book, *Harpers Ferry Under Fire, a Border Town in the American Civil War*, and the Laney Book Prize for *September Suspense, Lincoln's Union in Peril.* He was the recipient of the Shelby Foote Preservation Legacy Award from American Battlefield Trust and the Distinguished Service Award, the highest honor bestowed by the National Park Service.

Dennis and his wife Sylvia live in Burnside's post-battle headquarters on the outskirts of Sharpsburg with their two Boston Terriers, General Grant and Julia Dent Grant.

LM: What are you doing in your retirement?

DF: I'm not retired. I am no longer an employee of the National Park Service but I will never retire from my passion for history. I have been blessed my entire life in that my vocation and avocation have been one and the same. When I left my vocation—my professional historian role at Harpers Ferry—I slipped right into my avocation without missing a second. I love researching and writing, and especially love giving tours at the battlefields. Finding new approaches and new stories to tell keeps me fresh and keeps me young.

LM: How did growing up near Antietam shape your love of Civil War history? What were your early influences?

DF: Growing up in Pleasant Valley, midway between Harpers Ferry and Antietam, was very significant. I woke up every morning to the sun coming up over South Mountain at Crampton's Gap, a mile away from my home. I was completely surrounded and immersed by Civil War history at a very young age.

My father, John Frye (now 90), was the unofficial historian of Washington County for nearly 70 years. As a little boy, I would go along with him on his tours. I was fascinated by his presentations and intrigued

with the way he could take a place where history occurred and make it come to life as if the history was still happening.

In the sixth grade, I decided I was going to be a park ranger and nothing was going to stop me. I was going to dedicate all my free time to becoming a park ranger, so by the next year I was volunteering at the blacksmith's shop at Harpers Ferry and the Dunker Church at Antietam, doing interpretation and living history. The Dunker Church was easy because I am a Dunker. Some people were surprised that Dunkers still existed. I was the real thing.

Also at age 13, I was leading Washington County bus tours myself. People would get on the bus and say, "Where's the guide?" I would say, "He'll be along shortly," then as the bus pulled off, I would pick up the mic and introduce myself as the guide. I also did my first solo guide at Antietam that year. Antietam was my backyard, my home. My presentations were personal – I wanted to share the experience of living here with my tour groups. That gave me great advantage as a story teller and ultimately as a park ranger.

When I turned 18, I became a seasonal ranger at Harpers Ferry. I'll never forget the first time I put on the uniform. It was January 30, 1977. I stood in front of the hall mirror at my parents' home and gazed at myself because my dream was reflected in front of me. I still get chills thinking about that moment.

LM: What sparked your interest in battlefield preservation?

DF: Once again, I was influenced by my father. He is one of the founders of the Chesapeake and Ohio Canal National Historical Park. Though not on the original 1954 Douglas hike, Dad soon was walking the canal with Supreme Court Justice William O. Douglas, who was protesting a plan to convert the canal into a four-lane parkway that would run between Washington, D.C. and Cumberland, Maryland. My father helped build the coalition that fought that plan from 1958 until victory in 1971 when, against great odds and remarkable opposition, the canal became a national historical park. I grew up watching him fight that fight day in and day out.

Also, in 1966 my father went on the war path against a local power company's plan to build a power line through Washington County that would have been in direct view of most of the Antietam Battlefield and Pleasant Valley, crossing South Mountain near Crampton's Gap. Back then companies could do things like that without community input. My father exposed the power company and declared that "they were destroying history." He teamed up with a politically connected Harpers Ferry Road neighbor, Bernard Hildebrand (the power line intended to cross his farm near the Antietam Aqueduct on the C&O Canal), and together they convinced the Secretary of the Interior to use his authority under the newly-enacted National Historic Preservation Act, which requires the Federal Government to examine actions that might have an effect on federal property. In the end, the power company was forced to change its route. That was a great victory. When you stand anywhere on the battlefield today, it is nearly impossible to see that power line.

Dad's preservation battles were what I grew up with. I was destined to be a preservationist—it's in my genes. I didn't understand everything my father was doing at the time, but there was this almost spiritual osmosis occurring where he was instilling in me the values and methods to take on the big guys, save history, and be the winner. That is exactly the preservation method that I brought to the battlefield movement, which started in the mid-1980's.

LM: American Battlefield Trust refers to you as one of the founding fathers of the modern Civil War battlefield preservation movement, and you've won several awards for your work in preserving key battlefield lands. What are some of the results of your efforts that we can see today?

DF: By the mid-1980's Antietam had become one of the most threatened battlefields in the country. My attitude mirrored my father's, "Don't mess with my battlefield!" Things were happening that were going to screw up Antietam. I hadn't planned to create an organization at Antietam, but in 1985 only a fraction of the battlefield-and none of the historic land outside the battlefield-was protected. Developers were moving in. That's why we established the Save Historic Antietam Foundation (SHAF).

It started when the Washington County commissioners quietly rezoned the Grove Farm (historic farm where President Lincoln met with George McClellan after the Battle of Antietam) for the purpose of building a shopping center without first inquiring about the history of this site. When I found out, the first thing I did was contact two trusted friends and allies, Rev. John Schildt and Tom Clemens (long time Antietam guides, authors, and preservationists). The three of us became the founding members of SHAF and we went to war with the County Commissioners. After a bitter struggle involving legal action, SHAF purchased much of the property. With the help of the State of Maryland there are now permanent easements on the Grove farm.

I was careful not to mix my professional job at Harpers Ferry with my preservation passion for Antietam. All of that was done on my own time.

Concurrent with this experience, the National Trust for Historic Preservation launched a new program called "America's Top 11 Most Endangered Historic Places" to call attention to threatened historic sites across the country. Because SHAF had gotten national attention, the Trust was aware of us. SHAF lobbied successfully to have Antietam included on their first list. What we could not have hoped for was that they decided to list the 11 sites alphabetically, so Antietam appeared first -which many thought meant Antietam was the most threatened of the 11! Now we had unparalleled national attention, and something had to be done about Antietam. Even the private property inside the park boundary was zoned for agriculture, it was at stake because Washington County allows for one dwelling per acre on agricultural land. The Cornfield could have become a 30-house subdivision!

The best news of all was that Paul Mellon (of the Paul Mellon Foundation) learned about Antietam's threatened condition and provided Foundation money to purchase the Cornfield, West Woods, North Woods, land bordering Bloody Lane, and other parcels. Mellon became a champion for the protection of Antietam. Hence, because of the national attention brought by SHAF much of the battlefield was saved.

LM: What's your goal when giving battlefield tours?

DF: I want people to be provoked - think of Antietam, Harpers Ferry, South Mountain - in ways they haven't before. I know the tactics and details of the battles, but when I give my programs, they're not tactical. I tell people right up front that we're going to go up to the stratosphere and think about matters rather than examine maneuvers. The only time I discuss tactics is when an individual had an ancestor who fought at a particular part of the battlefield. That's a perfect time for a tactical discussion because it has personal meaning genetically to that visitor.

LM: As an historian, you are known for challenging convention. What are some of the discoveries you've made as a result of that approach?

DF: I consider myself a pioneer in terms of Civil War scholarship because I've uncovered and examined primary sources previously unexamined. I believe that traditional sources - manuscripts, diaries, journals, biographies, and so on - have pretty much been tapped out. Many of these primary sources are "filtered histories" – written long after the fact and clouded by memory. Sometimes they are fabricated purposely as memory to benefit the writer, which is human nature. Every once in a while, a new document or record is discovered, but for the most part Civil War history has become repetitive.

One of the ways I've contributed to Civil War scholarship and challenged convention is that I began exploring Civil War newspapers. Very rarely were newspapers cited as sources in Civil War scholarship. They've always been out there, but they weren't very accessible. Newspapers are immediate, primary sources. They give you glimpses and insights into the literal thinking and soul of the people at the time, unfiltered. I don't think you can get any closer to the Civil War experience than through the period newspapers, so that's what I began to explore. It has been an exciting adventure over the last 20 years to examine those sources. What made it possible was that repositories were digitized and placed on the Internet. I can sit here in Burnside's headquarters and read 1862 newspapers from all over the country. It's been a real revolution for me as an historian.

When the 150th anniversary of the first invasion of the North was coming up, I wanted to write a book. Do something that nobody else had done, something fresh and novel. I came up with the idea of using newspapers to find out what they, in September of 1862, were thinking and experiencing. I thought I knew a lot about Antietam, but as I wrote *September Suspense*, I discovered how much I didn't know because nobody had looked at the newspapers.

I've been blessed to have the talents and skills to be a researcher and writer. People often ask me which book is my favorite. I've written 11 books but I can't give you a favorite – that's like trying to say which of my dogs is my favorite. *September Suspense*, however, is unique in terms of Civil War scholarship because it reveals so much about the first invasion period that nobody else had explored. I feel it's a significant contribution.

LM: How did interpretation of Harpers Ferry's Civil War history change over the years you served as a park ranger at Harpers Ferry, ultimately as Chief Historian?

DF: After graduating from Shepherd University, I began working as a full-time supervisory ranger at Harpers Ferry. I could not have had a better start. I moved into the Master Armorer's house. Every morning I would look out my window and down on the John Brown Fort, the United States Arsenal and the water gap. Best of all, I was a park ranger in my own back yard. Back then, nobody at Harpers Ferry talked much about the Civil War. Every breath was John Brown, John Brown.

Then I had a ten-year interlude where I left the park service and worked in the private sector with non-profit organizations, such as the American Battlefield Trust. I also worked for Ted Turner and as a principal consultant and associate producer to Ron Maxwell, director of the movie *Gettysburg*. As we were making *Gods and Generals*, I helped bring that movie to Washington County for production.

When I came back into the NPS after a 10-year hiatus, the park had just obtained the School House Ridge Battlefield, hundreds of acres that were instrumental in the Confederate victory at Harpers Ferry. It was totally raw—there was no interpretation, no trails, no landscape improvements. The same with the Chambers-Murphy farm, which was another important property in the Confederate victory. All had been private property when I left in 1994. When I came back in 2004, it was public but not open nor accessible. I literally got to develop a battlefield from scratch. I helped design and lay out the trails, walking tours, exhibits, brochures, everything associated with opening a section of a national park.

Harpers Ferry is a model of battlefield preservation. When I started working there in the 1970's, not a square inch of the Confederate portion of the battlefield was in the national park. Now, virtually all of the Confederate battlefield is within the national park.

LM: In your opinion, what are the key takeaways related to the Maryland Campaign of 1862 for visitors to Harpers Ferry?

DF: An umbilical cord connects the battles of Harpers Ferry and Antietam. Without one we don't have the other. Harpers Ferry has always been in the shadow of Antietam, and Antietam deserves the extraordinary visibility that it receives. Antietam was an absolute turning point. But Antietam doesn't happen without Harpers Ferry, so you cannot separate the two.

Lee's first concern once the invasion was launched became Harpers Ferry. He was certain the United States forces would withdraw from the Shenandoah Valley, but when that didn't happen, he altered his plans considerably and directed two-thirds of his army to move against the Federal troops in the Shenandoah Valley and Harpers Ferry. This was no sideshow. It was the show. He did not want any Yankees in his rear because his intention was to get across the Mason-Dixon line into real Yankee country. Pennsylvania was where he wanted to meet the enemy. Pennsylvania is where the *real invasion* commenced.

Lee was delayed substantially as Confederate operations occurred in Harpers Ferry. According to Special Orders 191, the entire movement to Harpers Ferry was to be completed by September 12 and the army reunited. But Lee and Jackson underestimated the blockages that were going to slow them down, such as mountains, rivers, and the condition of the troops.

Special Orders 191 was discovered on September 13 - the day *after* Jackson's mission at Harpers Ferry was to be completed. So, it was old news! Except that it wasn't. Jackson was way behind and McClellan was moving much faster than Lee expected.

As a result of South Mountain, Lee withdrew, intending to cross the Potomac River into Virginia. Lee had canceled the invasion until receiving the message from Jackson that Harpers Ferry had capitulated. That's when he made the fateful decision to reunite his army at Sharpsburg. I did not state that Lee made a decision to "stand" or "fight" at Antietam. In my book, *Antietam Shadows*, I make it clear that the evidence suggests that Lee remained in Maryland so that he could unify his army with the full intention of heading north into Pennsylvania. There were only 15 miles between where he was at Sharpsburg and the Mason-Dixon Line, and nobody was there to block him.

But McClellan's flanking maneuver on September 16th blocked Lee's avenue north, which ultimately led to the battle. Lee's plan hinged on McClellan staying on the east bank of the Antietam Creek. That was a miscalculation.

LM: You and your wife have lovingly restored the house used by Ambrose Burnside as his post-Antietam headquarters. What challenges came with living in and restoring a pre-Civil War historic property?

DF: I was not afraid of the challenges because one of my responsibilities at Harpers Ferry was building restoration. I was well-schooled in that professional field and had an opportunity to do it privately, with my own house and my own money. There was no fear, but I understood that it would be costly and take a long time. The house had been vacant for a number of years. The poor thing looked like it had weeping eyes when I first saw it.

The house today has a beaming smile. I refer to myself as the caretaker, never as the owner. It's my job to make it better than when I found it, and to extend it to the next generation in the best condition I can make it. It's an honor to reside here in this fabulous house full of history.

President Lincoln conferenced with Burnside here on October 2, 1862 when he first arrived at Antietam. In fact, he met with Burnside before he met with McClellan. I often muse about that conversation and can almost hear the president say, "Now listen, McClellan needs to move, and if he doesn't, I'm going to remove him. And this time general, it won't be a request that you take command, it will be an order." Every morning when I go downstairs and walk on these original floorboards, I feel the presence of Lincoln and Burnside.

LM: What is your next major research project?

DF: There is no comprehensive book on the Battle of Harpers Ferry. I have nearly 50 years of materials on Harpers Ferry and I've never written that book. I think it's my job to write it, to promote Harpers Ferry as a Civil War battlefield. It wasn't thought of that way when I first arrived there in the 1970s. Everything was focused on John Brown.

I had a successful career of bringing Harpers Ferry out of the shadows and advancing it as a Civil War park, but I did that by writing lots of articles that have been published at the national level. That Battle of Harpers Ferry book keeps calling me. There is some reason only the Divine Creator knows that I had my entire career at Harpers Ferry. I think I would be happy to go to eternal life if the last thing I did here was complete my book on the Battle of Harpers Ferry. This book would epitomize my reason for being.

Book Reviews

Lyons, Brendan J. *Charley: The True Story of the Youngest Soldier to Die in the American Civil War.* Havertown, PA: Brookline Books, 2023. Soft cover, 160 pages. ISBN: 978-1955041065. $22.95.

Review by Kevin R. Pawlak

Of the more than 23,000 casualties suffered during the Battle of Antietam, none were younger than 13-year-old Charley King. This boy's death epitomizes the greater tragedy of the American Civil War. He was the youngest person killed in combat during the four years of the conflict.

Beyond contemporary newspaper articles and postwar regimental histories, King's story first came to the masses in a brief vignette of William Frassanito's 1978 book, *Antietam: The Photographic Legacy of America's Bloodiest Day.*

Since then, first-time author Brendan J. Lyons has worked tirelessly to ensure King's story is not forgotten. As an Eagle Scout, Lyons raised funds and a monument to King in a local cemetery in King's hometown. More recently, Lyons has written the first book dedicated to Charley's military life.

Lyons begins King's story in the earliest days of the Civil War in April 1861. He traces King's martial spirit early in the war and the debate with his parents about joining the Union army, something his parents refused to allow but ultimately relented when Capt. Benjamin Sweeney vowed to protect their son.

Charley: The True Story of the Youngest Soldier to Die in the American Civil War traces the boy's role and that of the 49th Pennsylvania throughout the early part of the war, from its camps outside of Washington, DC, to its service on the Virginia Peninsula and outside of Richmond in the summer of 1862. The book ends with King's untimely death on September 20, 1862, from wounds suffered at Antietam.

Throughout the book, Lyons uses the historical record to plug as many gaps in King's biography as possible, though the author admits that the parts of the story that are "not known, is from my heart and my desire to honor the life of Charley King, as well as the lives of the other valiant dead" (vi). The book is well written and does justice to King's life, but the lack of any notes makes it difficult–sometimes impossible–to discern

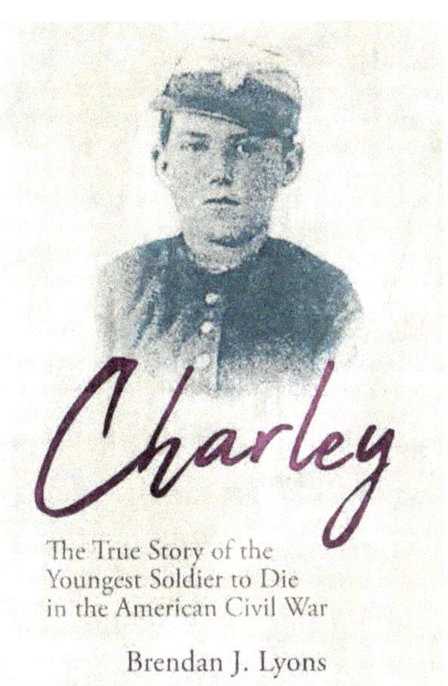

what is fact and what is a figment of the author's creation.

Nonetheless, Lyons' book will bring to light one of the Civil War's most tragic stories to young readers–its intended audience–and seasoned Civil War readers. Through his work, Lyons has done more than anyone else today to keep Charley's memory alive.

Contributor Biographies

Steven R. Stotelmyer is a native of Hagerstown, Maryland. He first visited Antietam National Battlefield as a child picnicking with his family in the Philadelphia Brigade Park. He has been fascinated with Antietam ever since. After serving in the U.S. Navy, he earned a Bachelor of Science degree from Frostburg State College and a Master of Arts from Hood College in Frederick. Mr. Stotelmyer was employed as a teacher in Washington County. The high point of the school year in the spring for his students was the all-day field trip to Antietam. After ten years teaching Steve made a career change into surveying, and civil engineering, in Frederick County. His daily commute took him over the South Mountain Battlefield. This travel, and the twenty-five years in "Fredericktowne" expanded his curiosity into the Maryland Campaign. He returned to Washington County and was employed by county government in the Public Works Department. Steve retired in 2014 and has since been pursuing his lifetime avocation at Antietam. In 1989 Stotelmyer was a founding member of the Central Maryland Heritage League, a non-profit land trust which helped preserve some of the South Mountain Battlefield. During his tenure with CMHL he discovered significant information regarding the Battle of South Mountain and the Legend of Wise's Well. This led to the publication of *The Bivouacs of the Dead: The Story of Those Who Died at Antietam and South Mountain* (Toomey Press, 1992). In 2019 Stotelmyer authored *Too Useful To Sacrifice, Reconsidering George B. McClellan's Generalship in the Maryland Campaign from South Mountain to Antietam.* (Savas Beatie, 2019). Currently, Steve is a National Park Service Volunteer as well as a NPS Certified Antietam and South Mountain Battlefield Tour Guide. His most recent book, *From Frederick to Sharpsburg: People, Places, and Events of the Maryland Campaign Before Antietam*, was recently published by the Antietam Institute.

Wilson H. Beebe Jr. first found his way to the study of Civil War memory and commemoration through *Patriotic Gore*, Edmund Wilson's writings on the literature of the period. Retired from his career as a trade association executive and lobbyist, his essays on the Antietam battlefield have developed out of his 30-year study of, periodic visits to, and particular appreciation for Antietam and the Maryland Campaign area. Married and a resident of Red Bank, New Jersey, he is a Navy veteran and holds a BA in English Literature from Fordham University.

James A. Rosebrock served in the United States Army for 28 years, retiring as a lieutenant colonel. He has volunteered at Antietam National Battlefield since 2007 and currently works with Antietam's artillery detachment, Battery B, 4th United States Artillery. An Antietam Battlefield Guide since 2009, Rosebrock led the guide service from 2012 to 2018. He is a founding member of the Antietam Institute and the author of *Artillery of Antietam.*

Brian Wyland is a student of all facets of the American Civil War with a strong interest in the units and individuals associated with the states of Minnesota and Wisconsin. This is his first article related to a historical topic. He works as a software professional and lives with his family in western Wisconsin.

J. O. Smith has a master's degree in history from the University of Georgia and undergraduate and law degrees from Duke University. He is an attorney and lives with his family near Annapolis, Maryland. He has been a Certified Antietam Battlefield Guide since 2018.

Laura L. Marfut is a retired U.S. Army colonel with master's degrees in International Relations and Education, and a Master of Strategic Studies degree from the U.S. Army War College. She has been a Certified Antietam Battlefield Guide since 2019.

Antietam Institute Membership Honor Roll

Corporate Members

Special thanks to all our Corporate Members!
Your support provides essential funding to help us sustain and grow educational programs and publications that are the foundation of the Institute.

Antietam Creek Vineyards
4835 Branch Ave
Sharpsburg, MD 21782
antietamcreekvineyard.com
240-490-2851

Antietam Mercantile Co.
138 W. Main Street
Sharpsburg, MD 21782
Facebook.com/AntietamMercantile
240-310-4011

Bonnie's at the Red Byrd
19409 Shepherdstown Pike
Keedysville, MD 21756
Facebook.com/Bonniesattheredbyrd
301-432-5822

Captain's Creations
311 Woodbury Avenue
Martinsburg, WV 25404
Facebook.com/CaptainsCreations
410-615-9213

Corporate Members

Captain Bender's Tavern
111 East Main Street
Sharpsburg, MD 21782
captainbenderstavern.com
301-432-5813

The Inn at Antietam
220 East Main Street
Sharpsburg, MD 21782
innatantietam.com
301-432-6601

Jacob Rohrbach Inn
138 W. Main Street
Sharpsburg, MD 21782
jacob-Rohrbach-inn.com
301-432-5079

Honor Guard Members
(Life-time members)
Wayne N. Blattner
Matt Borders
Mac Bryan
Jim Buchanan
Lucas Cade
Sharon Clough
Mike Crume
Ken Derrenbacher
Bruce Gorley
Brad Gottfried
Robert Gottschalk
Rogers M. Fred, III
Staci Fromwiller
Michael Hill
Clay Hoffman
Michael Kirschner
Laura L. Marfut
Mike McCartney
Mark McCurdy
Joseph McGraw
Colleen McMillan
Tom McMillan
Sharon Murray
Keith O'Neil
Kevin Pawlak
Scottie Riffle
Gary Rohrer
Jim Rosebrock
Robert Russo
Kate Shaffer
Austin Slater
Henry Stiles
Robert Strong
Frank Trotta
Clayton Tucker
Doug Valentine
Chris Vincent

Jeffrey Wilson
Darin Wipperman
Charles W. Young

Honorary Colonel Members
Joyce Burns-Schrage
Jay Ferris

Honorary Captain Members
Warren Breisblatt
Gordon Dammann
Richard Forziati
Judi McHugh
Sidney White

As of February 15, 2024

Antietam Institute Honor Roll
The Institute would like to recognize and again thank some special
contributors who have significantly supported the goals of the
organization.

2024
Gary Rohrer

2023
John Binau
James Clement
Mike Crume
Mark Davis
Paul Errett
William "Corky" Lowe
Mark McCurdy
Daniel Mick
Robert Occhiuti
Keith O'Neil
Ron Perisho
Rogers Fred III

Gary Rohrer
James Rosebrock
John Schildt
Frank Simpson
Doug Valentine
Chris & Amy Vincent
Janet Weeks

2022
David Boswell
Miriam Cunningham
Mark Fitsimmons
Judi McHugh
Gary Rohrer
Frank Simpson
Clayton Tucker
Sid White
J. Leonard Teti*
Joshua Pollack*
Christina & Steven Master*
Clayton Ramsey*

2021
Rogers Fred
Gary Rohrer

As of February 15, 2024

*—non-members who generously donated specifically to help fund the Institute scholarship at Shepherd University

Antietam Institute
2024 Membership Application

☐ **New Member**   ☐ **Renewal**

NAME: _________________________   HOME PHONE: (___) ___________

EMAIL ADDRESS: ___________________   CELL PHONE: (___) ___________

MAILING ADDRESS: ____

CITY: _______________   STATE: ___________   ZIP CODE: ___________

Preferred method of communication: ☐ email   ☐ phone   ☐ post

Please select your Membership Level (benefits are listed on reserves side form):

☐ Cadet - $10 (Student)
☐ Private - $25
☐ Corporal - $50
☐ Sergeant - $75
☐ *Sergeant Major - $150

☐ *Lieutenant - $250
☐ *Captain - $350
☐ *Colonel - $500
☐ *Honor Guard (Life Member) - $1000
☐ *Sutler – Business Member- $500

*Please select shirt size: SM ☐   MD ☐   LG ☐   XL ☐   2XL ☐   3XL ☐

Please select Style: Men's ☐   Women's ☐

PLEASE MAKE CHECK PAYABLE TO: Antietam Institute
P.O. Box 33
Sharpsburg, MD 21782

How did you hear about the Antietam Institute?

____

Through your membership the Antietam Institute will be able to support the Antietam National Battlefield and other local preservation and historical organizations. Your membership will also entitle you to attend Institute events as well as discounted publications and merchandise. The Institute is a tax-exempt, public benefit, non-profit corporation and qualifies under Section 501(c)(3) of the IRS code. Your membership and donations are tax-deductible as allowed by law.

If you have any questions or need additional information, contact our Membership at:
membership@antietaminstitute.org

Cadet - $10 (Student, under 21 in school)
• 10% discount on all Antietam Institute merchandise and events.

Private - $25
• 10% discount on all Antietam Institute merchandise

Corporal - $50
• Same benefits as Private Level • Subscription to our bi-annual "Antietam Journal"

Sergeant - $75
• Same benefits as Corporal Level • Antietam Institute logo hat

Sergeant Major - $150
• Same benefits as Sergeant Level • Antietam Institute logo polo shirt • *Exclusive offer - copy of **Commanders of Antietam** (available for a limited time only)

Lieutenant - $250
• Same benefits as Sergeant Major Level • 25% discount to the annual Symposium or Conference • *Exclusive offer - copy of **Commanders of Antietam** (available for a limited time only)

Captain - $350
• Same benefits as Lieutenant Level • 25% discount to the annual Spring Symposium • 25% discount to the annual Fall Conference • Recognition as an "Honorary Captain" member in the *"Antietam Journal"* • *Exclusive offer - copy of **Commanders of Antietam** (available for a limited time only)

Colonel - $500
• Same benefits as Captain Level • Invitations to exclusive programs (Annual Honor Guard Gathering) • Recognition as an "Honorary Colonel" member in the *"Antietam Journal"* • *Exclusive offer - copy of **Commanders of Antietam** (available for a limited time only)

Honor Guard-$1000 (Lifetime Member)
• 10% discount on all Antietam Institute merchandise • Subscription to our bi-annual "Antietam Journal" • Antietam Institute logo hat • Antietam Institute logo polo shirt • Invitations to exclusive programs (Annual Honor Guard Gathering) • Recognition as an "Honor Guard" member in the *"Antietam Journal"* • *Exclusive offer - copy of **Commanders of Antietam** (available for a limited time only)

Institute Sutler - Business Sponsor - $500
• Receive the Antietam Journal, hat and polo shirt:; Invitation to Honor Guard Gathering • ¼ page advertisement in the "Antietam Journal" and in Institute event programs • Recognition and company logo on the Antietam Institute website. • Recognition as an "Honorary Sutler" in the "Antietam Journal"